Student Options

Editor: Danielle Lobban

Volume 403

independence
educational publishers

First published by Independence Educational Publishers

The Studio, High Green

Great Shelford

Cambridge CB22 5EG

England

© Independence 2022

Copyright

Photocopy licence

ISBN-13: 978 1 86168 862 0

Printed in Great Britain

Zenith Print Group

Contents

Introduction

Student Options is Volume 403 in the **issues** series. The aim of the series is to offer current, diverse information about important issues in our world, from a UK perspective.

STUDENT OPTIONS

Making choices for your future whilst at school can be a daunting prospect. In this book we look at some of the options available to you, as well as things such as making the best of revision, coping with exam stress and what you can do after school and beyond.

OUR SOURCES

Titles in the **issues** series are designed to function as educational resource books, providing a balanced overview of a specific subject.

The information in our books is comprised of facts, articles and opinions from many different sources, including:

♦ Newspaper reports and opinion pieces

♦ Website factsheets

♦ Magazine and journal articles

♦ Statistics and surveys

♦ Government reports

♦ Literature from special interest groups.

A NOTE ON CRITICAL EVALUATION

Because the information reprinted here is from a number of different sources, readers should bear in mind the origin of the text and whether the source is likely to have a particular bias when presenting information (or when conducting their research). It is hoped that, as you read about the many aspects of the issues explored in this book, you will critically evaluate the information presented.

It is important that you decide whether you are being presented with facts or opinions. Does the writer give a biased or unbiased report? If an opinion is being expressed, do you agree with the writer? Is there potential bias to the 'facts' or statistics behind an article?

ASSIGNMENTS

In the back of this book, you will find a selection of assignments designed to help you engage with the articles you have been reading and to explore your own opinions. Some tasks will take longer than others and there is a mixture of design, writing and research-based activities that you can complete alone or in a group.

FURTHER RESEARCH

At the end of each article we have listed its source and a website that you can visit if you would like to conduct your own research. Please remember to critically evaluate any sources that you consult and consider whether the information you are viewing is accurate and unbiased.

Useful Websites

www.anxietyuk.org.uk

www.careerpilot.org.uk

www.gov.uk

www.icould.com

www.inews.co.uk

www.nationalcareers.service.gov.uk

www.oxbridgehomelearning.uk

www.savethestudent.org

www.successatschool.org

www.theconversation.com

www.themix.org.uk

www.thetutorwebsite.co.uk

www.theuniguide.co.uk

www.topuniversities.com

www.whatuni.com

www.youthemployment.org.uk

Education in the UK

Differences between the curriculums and qualifications explained...

Education in most of the UK is broadly the same, with a few small exceptions. Scotland follow a different curriculmn and qualification system.

Secondary education (11-18 years)

Learners in England, Northern Ireland and Wales all follow their own curriculums, but they share Key Stages. They will also sit GCSE exams at the end of their secondary education.

Key Stage 3 is for ages 11-14 and Key Stage 4 is for ages 14-16.

GCSE stands for General Certificate of Secondary Education and are level 2 qualifications. Most learners will start studying for their GCSEs in Year 9 or 10, depending on the subject, school and exam board. Most learners will take around nine subjects.

After this learners will move on to sixth form or college to do A levels (also known as General Certificate of Education). These are level 3 qualifications. Usually you will choose three or four subjects that you will study over two years in more depth than the subjects studied in secondary school.

Scotland follows the Curriculum for Excellence and the qualifications and education stages are different than the rest of the UK.

Secondary schools are usually known as high schools or academies. The stages are S1 to S6 (equivalent in the rest of the UK is Years 8-13). National 5s (similar to GCSEs) are sat in S4, followed by Scottish Highers (similar to the old AS Levels) are sat in S5. Then, in the final year S6, students will take Scottish Advanced Highers (similar to A-Levels).

18+ education

Students who go on to higher education can choose from a variety of options, such as an apprenticeship, traineeship, undergraduate degree and many more.

In England, Northern Ireland and Wales, standard undergraduate courses last three years, while in Scotland they are four years long.

Costs can vary, so it's best to check with the university or course provider and finance may be available depending on your circumstances.

How important are GCSEs?

By Natasha Boydell

When you're 16, GCSEs can seem like the be all and end all. By the time you've been working for a few years, you've probably forgotten all about them and are wondering whether to even include them on your CV.

It's a commonly asked question – do people really care about GCSE results?

And the answer is, it depends. If you've had a successful 20-year career in your industry and you're applying to be the CEO of a major company, they're not going to give a hoot about whether you flunked GCSE art.

But if you're applying for your first job, then your CV will be pretty sparse and less likely to hide your GCSE sins. So it's safe to say that your grades become less important the older you get. Think of them as a gatekeeper – holding the key to the next stage in your education or career.

Put simply, good GCSE grades give you more options to choose from.

If you're currently (supposed to be) studying, here are some things to consider before you close your books and reach for your games console:

GCSEs can determine what you study at A-level

For many subjects, you need to pass them at GCSE in order to study them at A-level and, consequently, higher levels (like a degree) too.

There are exceptions – for example economics or law, but it's definitely worth checking with your teacher.

GCSEs can determine what sixth form you go to

Schools and colleges only really have your GCSE grades to judge you academically so they can be really important here.

According to Which, sixth forms see your GCSE performance as an indicator of how well you'll do in your A-levels or other, advanced studies, and use a scoring system based on your grades to predict how well you are likely to do.

All schools and colleges have entry requirements, which can vary from four to five Bs or Cs to straight As. So if you've got your heart set on going to a certain sixth form you should know what grades you'll need to get in.

You don't want to be the one whose mum has to drive you to a random college an hour away where you don't know anyone, while all your friends are hanging out and having lunch together at the nearby one.

Universities look at your GCSE grades

As a general rule, most universities expect at least some Cs at GCSE, especially in maths, English and, sometimes, science.

Many ask for, and expect, higher grades. However, don't despair – some universities aren't as hung up on GCSEs as others and, as long as you make up for it in your A-levels, you could well be absolutely fine.

For example, according to an article in *The Guardian*, Cambridge has no GCSE requirements except for medicine and veterinary medicine, where you have to have a grade C or above in GCSE double award science and maths.

Are GCSE grades important for apprenticeships?

Some apprenticeships require you to have certain grades at GCSE. For example, most advanced apprenticeships ask for around five GCSEs at grades A*-C, including English and maths.

But for some intermediate apprenticeships or traineeships, you don't need to have certain grades at all – instead, you may just need to show that you have the skills through things like work experience and volunteering.

You can find out more and search for apprenticeships on the government's apprenticeship website.

How important are GCSEs in getting a job?

Most employers expect people to have good Maths and English GCSEs and without this, it can be hard to get your foot in the door. In fact, this is so important that students who don't get a grade C or above in these subjects now have to carry on studying them until they are 18.

Most graduate schemes and school leaver programmes will have minimum GCSE grade requirements too.

However, there are other routes into getting jobs – for example, there are so many apprenticeships out there these days and, like we said above, some of these don't have any GCSE requirements.

What if I don't get the GCSE grades I was expecting?

Don't panic if you don't get the GCSE grades you were expecting.

We've spent most of the blog telling you why GCSEs ARE important. However, that doesn't mean that it's the end of the world if you don't get the grades you were hoping for.

If you haven't made the grade, or you're worried that you won't, please don't panic – you do have options.

They include contacting your school or college to see if they'll still accept you, resitting your exams, applying for a different course or doing an apprenticeship.

The above information is reprinted with kind permission from Success At School.
© 2022 Success At School

www.successatschool.org

What is a GCSE pass now? Number grades explained – and what to do if you fail English or maths

GCSE students are graded on a numerical system from 9 to 1, rather than grades from A to E.

By Sam Tabahriti

Students are graded on a numerical system from 9 to 1, rather than from A to E, after the system changed from letters to numbers in 2018.

Ofqual believes the numerical grading system helps to better differentiate between students and their abilities.

The exam body says that in theory there will be fewer 9s as 9, 8 and 7 all correspond to the top grades of A* and A, separating students at the top end of the spectrum.

In a normal year, GSCE grades in most subjects are dependent on exams but this year, as was the case in 2020, pupils have not sat exams due to the pandemic.

Instead, their teachers have been given the responsibility to award grades.

But what are the new grades?

The numerical grading scheme was brought in at the same time as a new GCSE curriculum in England.

The highest grade awarded is 9, with the lowest being 1, not including ungraded marks (U).

To help better differentiate the top grades, 9, 8 and 7 correspond to the previous top grades of A* and A.

The numerical grades were designed by former Education Secretary Michael Gove as a way to counter grade inflation at the top end, with A and A* grades now split between three result brackets.

A 4 is broadly being compared to a C grade, although Ofqual warns against 'direct comparisons and overly simplistic descriptions'.

It says that, broadly, the same proportion of teenagers will get a grade four and above as used to get a grade C or above.

What is a GCSE pass now?

Pupils previously needed a C grade in order to pass a GCSE exam. The new grading scheme has two pass marks – a standard pass is 4 and a strong pass is 5.

This means that students who get 4s across all modules will pass their exams.

However, many sixth forms will require a minimum of 5s and 6s as a condition of entry.

What if you fail Maths or English?

Appeal your grades

Due to the unprecedented circumstances caused by the pandemic, there has been quite some focus on making sure students aren't at a disadvantage due to Covid-19.

Pupils can appeal grades through their school as individual establishments will have their own processes.

Resit your exams

Should students fail Maths or English, meaning getting a grade below 4, resitting is compulsory.

If a student wants a higher mark than a pass in Maths and English – 4 or above – they may have the possibility to resit an exam.

When can I resit Maths and English?

Students who achieved a grade 1, 2, or 3, or who are unhappy with their grade, can choose to sit an examination in the autumn term.

Pupils have the opportunity to resit GSCE exams in November 2021, including in Maths and English.

Should they need more time to study, students also have the possibility to resit exams in January 2022.

Students will again have the possibility to appeal or ask for a remark if unhappy with their resit results.

Will schools and colleges still accept me if I failed a course?

To study A-Levels, generally students need a minimum of five GCSEs graded between 4 and 9, including Maths and English.

Pupils who fail one or two subjects should still find they are accepted on courses, as most schools and colleges will let people study GCSEs alongside A-Levels.

12 August 2021

Choosing your GCSE options

Starting work may seem a long way off, but the subjects you study now can make a real difference to your future. Check out our guide to choosing your options.

What's the deal?

♦ In year 9, you can select some of the subjects you would like to study in years 10 and 11. This is called choosing your options

♦ Everyone has to study maths, English and science, usually at GCSE-level

♦ The other subjects you can take will depend on your school. You should be able to choose at least one course from each of the following areas: arts (such as music and drama), design and technology; humanities (such as history and geography); and modern foreign languages. Sometimes you can also choose new subjects, such as law or sociology

♦ Alongside GCSEs, you can study for work-related qualifications, also called vocational qualifications or Technical Awards. They can help you develop practical skills in subjects such as construction, computing and childcare.

Why does it matter?

You'll be studying the subjects you choose for the next two years, and it's no fun being stuck with ones you don't really like.

Decisions you make now may limit your choices later so look ahead. What do want to do after year 11? Can this help you decide which subjects to choose?

Keeping your future options open

Exploring what subjects you may need in future is well worth the effort now. If you want to study certain subjects at A-level, you may need to have a GCSE in the subject first. To apply to certain university courses, you'll need certain A-levels. On the other hand, you can start some subjects from scratch, at both A-level and university.

Choosing a balance of subjects can help to keep your options open. The English Baccalaureate (EBacc) is a measure for schools which shows how many students take a number of set subjects (English, maths, history or geography, the sciences and a language) and their average results. EBacc subjects can prove a useful guide when choosing your options, especially if you want to continue with your studies.

What to think about

Take time to think things through.

♦ Consider which subjects you are good at, are interested in or enjoy

♦ Find out how courses are marked. If you don't like exams, you may prefer some subjects which include coursework, such as art or drama

♦ Look at the topics you'll be studying to get a flavour of the course. But beware – it's often tricky to tell if you'll like something you've not studied before!

♦ If you're trying to choose between two subjects, think about how each option fits with your other GCSEs. Does a subject go well with your other choices? Or does a subject provide a welcome change? If you're taking lots of essay-based subjects, it can be nice to include one choice with a more practical focus.

Who can help?

Talk to a range of people to get different views.

♦ Ask your subject teachers, form tutor, or careers teachers for advice

♦ Talk to your parents, carers or relatives

♦ Look out for special options assemblies or evenings at school

♦ Read any information or handouts you are given

♦ Speak to a careers adviser for free on the phone or online at the National Careers Service.

20 October 2021

Which GCSEs should you take? A guide to choosing subjects

In England, most students will choose the GCSE subjects that they want to study in year nine, when they're between thirteen and fourteen years old. GCSEs are then studied over the following two years leading to final exams. The majority of students will study nine or ten GCSEs, which is a credible number of qualifications for colleges, universities, and employers. Although, some academically advanced and ambitious students may take eleven or twelve GCSEs at a time. Why does this matter? Well, it depends on what career you have in mind. Taking triple science is recommended if you want to become a doctor, but it means you'll end up studying more than ten subjects. And universities sometimes favour students who have a wide range of subjects under their belt, to show that they are well-rounded learners. When you choose your subjects, you're shaping the beginning of your education, but also the direction of your life. They're the starting point for further learning, so whilst they might not be the golden ticket to your dream career, they give you the chance to head towards it.

For mature students looking to retake GCSEs later in life, picking their subjects is usually based on whether they need to achieve better grades, or study a different subject to meet the requirements of a new career. Most further education courses and jobs require you to have grades between 9 and 4 (or A* and C, if you're used to the old grading system) in a minimum of five subjects. So, whether you're in school, or an adult returning to learning, it's important to pick the right courses that you can both do well in, and use in the future. This guide to choosing GCSE subjects will give you the most relevant advice for ambitious students like you!

10 tips for choosing your GCSE subjects

1. Figure out which subjects are compulsory

In the UK, there are 'core' and 'foundation' subjects that all key stage 4 students must take. Maths, English, and science are the core subjects, and IT/computing, physical education, and citizenship are the foundations. In some cases, science can be split into two or three subjects, biology, chemistry, and physics, depending on the ability of the student. From there, most students will choose three or four optional courses based on their personal interests and further education plans.

2. Find out what options you have

There are four categories that all schools must offer at least one subject in. These categories are:

1. Modern foreign languages. Generally, schools will offer the most popular courses, such as French, German, and Spanish, though some schools might teach more complex languages, such as Mandarin and Russian. You should check whether taking a language GCSE is compulsory at your school, too.

2. Humanity subjects. This covers history, geography, religious studies, and the social sciences such as psychology and sociology.

3. Artistic subjects. These include music, drama, art and design, and media studies.

4. Technical subjects. This could be design and technology, food technology, and computer science.

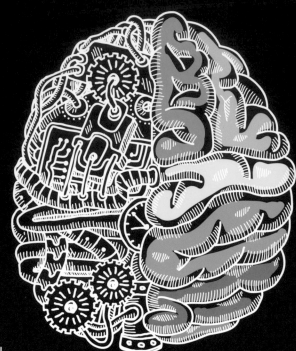

Left
- Verbal
- Analytical
- Orderly
- Logic
- Sequencing
- Linear thinking
- Mathematics
- Facts
- Thinking in words

Right
- Imagination
- Holistic thinking
- Intuition
- Arts
- Rhythm
- Non-verbal cues
- Visual thinking
- Daydreaming
- Adventurous

Source: Oxbridge

Some students have the option to choose a work-related qualification, and these are usually new subjects that are not studied at key stage three, for example, health and social care or business studies.

3. Focus on your passions and aspirations

Gaining a qualification in a subject that you don't enjoy is no use to you if it means your grades suffer as a result. What's more, if you're not passionate about the subject, chances are, you're not going to follow that path in the future. Learning should be a propellor for your personal development and career aspirations, so the most important thing you can do is pick the subjects that you're interested in! What fuels your curiosity? What motivates you? What ideas and concepts are you fascinated by? It doesn't matter if you're not sure what type of work you desire, as long as you understand that certain subjects are pathways into certain industries. For example, if you know you like being around people and think you could work in the social sector, taking a humanities subject, like sociology or psychology, alongside a modern language, such as French, would be useful.

4. Think of good subject combinations and strike a balance

Now, whilst we just said you should pick the subjects you like, it's also important to strike a balance between 'soft' and 'hard' subjects, so that universities can see how varied your abilities are. A 'hard' subject is another way of describing what's called a facilitating subject – those preferred by universities when applying for a range of degrees. This includes core subjects like maths and English, but also the three natural sciences, modern foreign languages, and things like economics and politics. 'Soft' subjects are generally more hands-on, practical, or vocational, for example, photography, media studies, art and design, drama, and the social sciences. Whilst it's more important to consider this when you're choosing your A-level subjects

because hard subjects are compulsory for GCSEs anyway, it's good to have that pathway in mind when selecting your optional courses. A balance between technical, academic, and practical subjects demonstrates that you're a well-rounded learner.

5. Review your skillset and strengths

Do you feel confident solving problems and equations? Or do you feel more comfortable communicating ideas? Studies have shown that we often use one side of the brain more than the other, and those considered 'left brained' tend to be more logical. Whilst people who are 'right brained' are more creative. However, that's not to say that you can't train the brain to use both these skills efficiently. It simply indicates what style of thinking you're more naturally dominant in. Knowing your strengths and learning styles will help when thinking about the subjects you'd be good at.

You should also research how different subjects are marked, and ask yourself, 'Is this GCSE largely coursework based, or exam-focused'? If you're the type of person that performs better under pressure, a subject marked solely under exam conditions would be fine. However, most students prefer subjects that have a mix of graded coursework and exams, so they can spend longer working on their assignments.

6. Seek guidance from a careers adviser

We know, we know. If you're in year nine, or even year eight, then you're still very young to be thinking about what job you want. And the fact is that throughout life, most adults switch jobs every five years on average anyway. So, we're not suggesting that you need to have it all figured out, or that what you decide is set in stone. However, it's good to know your options so you can get a feel for the kind of work you might be interested in.

A careers adviser can assess your interests, skills, and goals,

and help you decide what the most relevant subjects would be for you. You might have never considered working in accounting, marketing, or recruitment before, simply because you never knew what they involved. The best thing to do at this stage is to learn about and consider all possibilities so that you can narrow down the GCSEs that keep your options open.

If you're a mature student returning to education to re-take your GCSEs, we're pretty sure you already have a career path in mind. However, you might not know exactly what qualifications you need to get there. A quick chat with us will help to point you in the right direction.

7. Don't be influenced by others

If you're still at school, it's easy to be tempted by the subjects your friends have chosen, so you can be in the same classes. But whilst school is a social environment, classrooms are for learning! So, whether the GCSEs you pick are popular or not, they will have a huge impact on your future and your friends should have no influence on your decision. On top of that, don't let your parents tell you what courses to study either. You're the one that has to spend two years learning about the subject, and it's your life that it will impact in the long run.

8. Plan a realistic schedule that you can keep up with

Some subjects will clash on a school timetable, so you need to check if you can make all the classes for the subjects you've chosen. Say you're taking triple science as well as all the core subjects, and you've chosen four other GCSEs, you'll have twelve different classes to attend across the week. Make sure it's do-able and achievable; you don't want to be feeling stressed because you took on too many subjects or you're having to catch up with missed classes. If you're going to be online learning, be sure to plan a schedule that

fits alongside your other commitments. Plan a timetable that isn't too overwhelming but realistic to achieve the recommended study hours per course.

9. Think about how your GCSEs will complement your A-level choices

Some A-level courses will require you to have already achieved the same subject at GCSE level, so that you have the foundation knowledge to develop upon. For example, universities often value students who study A-level languages, such as French, but you'd need French GCSE first – that's if the subject is not your first language.

10. Understand that nothing is final, and you can still gain further GCSEs later in life

If there's one thing we know as an online college, it's that learning is lifelong! You can study your GCSEs, go on to achieve A-levels, go to university, and be happy in your job for ten years, until you decide you want to become a nurse and you didn't get a good enough maths GCSE to begin training. So, you find a course and you commit to studying again. Life will take you on many unexpected journeys, but education will only ever propel you forwards. Therefore, remember, nothing is final, and whilst the GCSEs you choose are important, they're not your only chance at success. Enjoy the ride.

We hope our guide to choosing GCSE subjects helped you figure out what courses are right for you.

What are your vocational options at GCSE level?

Looking for an alternative to GCSEs? You have a lot of vocational options that you can do as well as your core GCSEs like Maths...

By Jess Amy Dixon

Choosing your GCSE subjects can be a scary time. You might be wondering how to decide, what to do if you make the wrong choice, and whether these decisions will impact the rest of your life.

First: don't panic!

GCSE subjects are important, but they can't and won't define the rest of your life. And if you start doing one subject and quickly realise it's not right for you, many schools will let you swap to another subject.

Today we're looking at one of the options you might be wondering about: vocational GCSEs and GCSE equivalents.

What are vocational qualifications?

There are some subjects GCSE students have to take, including English and Maths. Some schools also have their own requirements, such as requiring students to take a language subject. But apart from that, you get to choose your own options. Most students take around 9 GCSEs or equivalent.

In short, vocational qualifications are those that are practical and directly related to a specific job or career path. A vocation is just another word for a job or career.

Most vocational subjects offer a mix of theoretical and hands-on learning, allowing you to get a good foundational understanding of the subject while also getting plenty of actual experience.

What types of qualifications are available?

At GCSE level, those interested in vocational qualifications have three main options to choose from.

♦ **GCSEs in vocational subjects.** Most GCSEs are more academic and theoretical, but a small number of vocational subjects are available. They include Business, IT, Computer Science, and Engineering.

♦ **OCR Cambridge Nationals.** These are designed for students aged 14-16, just like GCSEs. They take two years of study to complete. Some of the subjects available include Child Development, Engineering, ICT, and Sport Science.

♦ **BTEC First Diploma.** BTEC qualifications are available at many different levels, and taken by students from age 14 all the way up to adults. A BTEC First Diploma is the equivalent to 4 GCSEs. Subjects you can study include Music, Performing Arts, Sport, and Business.

I just don't want to make the wrong decision!

Dearest, whatever path you choose we'll support you.

Not all schools will offer all of these, so you'll need to explore what's available at your school – or consider switching schools if that's the best thing for you.

Who are vocational GCSEs and similar qualifications for?

Vocational GCSEs and GCSE alternatives are ideal for those who have a good idea of what job or employment sector they want to go into, and want to start preparing for the world of work or further job based training.

If you're a practical and hands-on person who learns best by doing, you are likely to thrive on a vocational course.

It's important to note that vocational qualifications aren't necessarily easier than GCSEs. They're still a rigorous programme of study and you'll be expected to work hard, complete homework, and prepare for your final exams or assessments. They're a different kind of qualification, and one that works better for some people.

What can I do after I've completed a vocational GCSE or equivalent?

Vocational GCSEs or other vocational qualifications leave you with lots of great options! So don't worry if you're not sure what you want to do next. Here are a few options you might want to consider:

♦ **Further study.** For example, you might choose to take A Levels or other subject specific qualifications. A Levels are academic qualifications, but there are also many vocational equivalents on offer. For example, you might choose to study for a higher level BTEC qualification, or take another type of qualification such as T Levels. At some schools and colleges, you can take a mix of academic and vocational subjects.

♦ **Apprenticeship.** In an apprenticeship scheme, you work for an employer and train for a qualification at the same time. It gives you real, on-the-job experience and lets you earn a wage while you study. In many apprenticeship programmes, you'll need to go to college part time – usually one day per week. Apprenticeships are available in an enormous array of trades, from hair and beauty to plumbing, IT, and construction.

♦ **Go to work.** Your vocational GCSEs or equivalents will put you in a great position to get a job when you leave school.

Can I do a vocational GCSE even if I'm not sure of my career plans?

Absolutely!

Here's something you might not realise: a lot of people don't know what future career they want to do when they're 14. And many more change their minds. So don't think you have to have your entire life planned out to make good GCSE choices. You don't!

At this stage, the most important thing to do is to identify your strengths.

Every GCSE, both academic and vocational, gives you transferable skills that you can use in other areas of work, life, and study. So even if you don't end up working in that particular field, your qualification will never be a waste.

Get some advice

Still confused about your GCSE options? There is plenty of support out there, so ask for some help and advice. Talk to your parents or guardian, a trusted teacher, your school's careers expert, or an older sibling or friend who has been there. They all want you to succeed.

Whatever you decide, good luck – we know you'll smash it!

26 February 2021

A-levels and AS-levels, explained

Confused about how your AS-level and A-level studies are structured? We clear up what you'll study (and when).

By Andy Gardner, Careers Adviser

What is an A-level?

An 'advanced level' or A-level is a qualification offered across a range of subjects to school-leavers (usually aged 16-18 years old), graded A*-E.

A-levels are studied across two years: your AS year (Year 12) and your A2 year (Year 13).

You can read more about how A-levels work, below.

The way A-levels work has changed in recent years – students used to take ongoing module assessments to determine their final grade, but these days 100% of students' grades are decided by their final exams.

You may hear A-levels being described as 'linear' – this is to reflect this change in how they are assessed.

What are linear A-levels?

AS-levels and A-levels have been 'decoupled', which means your overall A-level grades now depend solely on exams you take at the end of your second year (for the most part – there are some exceptions).

Previously, marks that you achieved for a subject in your AS year could be 'banked' and carried over, to contribute to your A-level grade. For those who aren't keen on exams, sadly this is no longer the case.

What is an AS-level?

This simply refers to the first year of a full A-level.

You can study a subject for one year and achieve an AS-level qualification that's independent from those subjects you carry on with to the full A-level. Most students who decide to take an extra AS-level do it in their first year, so they can focus 100% on their A-levels in their second year.

When you decide to continue an AS subject into your A2 year, you're pursuing it further for the full A-level qualification.

Do AS-levels count as A-levels?

While you will take exams for all your subjects at the end of your AS year, your AS marks can't be banked towards your final A-level grade..

For the subjects you carry on with the following year: while your AS-level grades still matter, they won't contribute to your final A-level grades a year later. Instead, you'll have to sit the final A-level exams.

For the subject you drop: these marks will decide your grade for what will be your AS-level qualification.

Note, the above only applies in England. In Wales and Northern Ireland, your AS-level marks can still be banked and carried over to count towards (40% of) your final A-level grade.

Your AS-levels do matter

That AS-level qualification for the subject you've dropped is still important in its own way.

Whatever UCAS points this translates to may still contribute to the total points you apply to university with. AS-levels are now equal to 40% of an A-level. For example, an A-level A grade is worth 48 UCAS points and an AS-level A grade is worth 20.

Your teachers will also decide your predicted grades based on your AS-level performance in these subjects, which in turn will impact your university application.

Can I take an AS-level?

Schools and colleges are not legally obliged to offer AS-levels and enter students for the relevant exams, so not everywhere will offer them.

When choosing your A-levels – including whether you want to stay at your school to study them, or go elsewhere – check what options the institution offers.

What A-level subjects can you study?

There are around 80 different subjects available to study at A-level. However, the options available to you will depend on what your school or college offers.

Typical A-level subjects include:

♦ Ones you've studied before: history, music, chemistry etc.

♦ Variations on ones you've studied before: eg you could choose between English literature, English language, or English literature and language; or you could take maths and further maths.

♦ Subjects you've never had the chance to study before: eg law, philosophy, psychology etc.

What do you need to study A-levels?

Schools and colleges will often look for at least five GCSEs 9-4 (or A*-C under the old grading system), or equivalent.

English, maths and sometimes science are the important subjects to get these grades in – not just when applying to A-levels, but to university and jobs too – as well as any subjects you plan to study at A-level.

While a C/4 is a minimum, higher GCSE grades will leave you in a better position.

How do A-levels work?

Your AS year (Year 12)

You'll typically choose three or four subjects to take.

Some students take more subjects, if they're planning to apply to a competitive university (eg Oxford, Cambridge) or course (eg medicine, law), for example. Most universities'

A-level entry requirements boil down to three A-level grades.

At the end of the year, you take exams in all your subjects. The relevance of your results depend on whether you're dropping it (if so, this will decide your AS-level grade, if your school offers these) or carrying it on (in which case, this will bear no impact on your final A-level grade, but could shape your predicted grades).

The grade you achieve in any AS-level will still go on your Ucas application, (along with your predicted A-level grades).

Your A2 Year (Year 13)

You'll continue with your remaining subjects to achieve the full A-level.

At the end of Year 13, your all-important exams will decide your final A-level grades. These will test you on content from both years.

Depending on the offers you receive, your actual A-level grades will determine whether you'll be heading straight off to uni, going through Clearing or taking a different path altogether.

You could pick up an additional AS-level subject this year, if, for example, you didn't take an AS-level in your first year or you need to boost the number of Ucas points when applying to university. Keep in mind that you'll have to juggle this along with your three A-level subjects in this 'all-or-nothing' year. Fast-forward to exam season and you might regret doing this…

Can I study BTECs with A-levels?

Yes, you can – this article goes into more detail about taking a BTEC with A-levels, including advice from students who've done it about how to juggle the qualifications.

Your decision to study a combination of A-levels and BTECs will depend on a few things, particularly what you plan to do afterwards. While BTECs allow students to acquire practical and vocational skills as part of the course, some universities and courses may have qualification preferences they look for. They'll state clearly what they look for in their entry requirements.

Do you still get A-levels with coursework?

A-levels are now primarily assessed by exams, which take place at the end of your second year. You'll still take exams at the end of your first year, but these won't count towards your final A-level grades.

Some subjects will be the exception to this, including:

◆ art and design, which understandably involves coursework projects you work on throughout the year;

◆ chemistry, biology, and physics, which include a practical element throughout the course.

What can you do after A-levels?

Here are some ideas:

◆ **Apply for university.** Search for a course to see what entry requirements universities ask for and see what A-levels are essential for different degrees. If you're not sure what you want to study, drop your A-levels into our Explorer to see the full breadth of degree subject possibilities available.

◆ **Keep your options open** with a foundation degree, Higher National Diploma or Higher National Certificate. These are shorter – just one or two years in duration – and can be 'topped up' to a full degree later if you wish.

◆ If you want a degree but without the fees, **consider the higher or degree apprenticeship route.** This combines university study with real work experience in a company.

◆ **Jump straight into paid employment.** You can apply to jobs that offer or support additional training, allowing you to progress further in the organisation.

18 November 2021

Scottish Highers: what are they and how many should I study?

We've got all the answers to your frequently asked questions about Scottish Highers...

By Holly Sawyer

There are multiple pathways into higher education, and these can differ depending on where you live in the UK. For those in England, A-Levels or BTECs are the most popular options. But, for those in Scotland, Scottish Highers are the go-to option for most.

But what exactly are Scottish Highers and if you want to go to university, how many do you need to study? Here's the answers you need...

What are Scottish Highers?

Simply put, Scottish Highers are the Scottish equivalent to A-Levels. They are courses that students aged 16-18 in Scotland sit that can lead to university, further study, training or work. You normally take on four to five Highers and start them in the fifth year of secondary school. Highers can also be sat in sixth form too alongside advanced Highers, explained further below.

Scottish Highers involve a mix of work set and marked by teachers and an external examination.

What's the difference between Scottish Highers and A-Levels?

Scottish Highers and A-Levels are very similar but are not identical - the location of students taking them being the most obvious difference. Another difference is that Scottish Highers are one-year courses, unlike A-Levels which take two. Scottish students can use a second year of study to complete Advanced Highers, which are an additional qualification.

Despite Scottish Highers only taking one year to complete, they offer plenty of UCAS points:

- ♦ A= 33 points
- ♦ B = 27 points
- ♦ C = 21 points
- ♦ D = 15 points

Advanced Highers offer:

- ♦ A = 56 points
- ♦ B = 48 points
- ♦ C = 40 points
- ♦ D = 32 point

This is in comparison to A-Levels, which offer:

- ♦ A* = 56 points
- ♦ A = 48 points
- ♦ B =40 points
- ♦ C = 32 points
- ♦ D = 24 points

Students in Scotland also get a much smaller range of subjects to study – 72 courses are on offer, whereas English counterparts get 123 A-Level choices in total.

How many Highers do I need to get into university?

In general, students need to get around four Highers to be accepted into university. This depends on the course you are applying for, but overall four Highers are required.

For the more competitive degrees, the grade requirements will be tougher – ideally 5 Highers will be achieved, then any additional qualifications from the second year of studying (the second year provides students with the chance to catch up on any lost grades in their first year, or study some Advanced Highers).

If you get the Highers and grades needed for Uni in one year of study, you may get some unconditional offers.

What are Advanced Highers?

If pupils pass higher courses in their first year of study, they can then go on to study for advanced Highers in an additional year. The average amount of advanced Highers students sit are two or three. Advanced Highers aren't needed to get into universities in Scotland, but they look good and help students' get an unconditional offer.

How should I choose my Scottish Highers?

If you're struggling to pick your Highers, there's a couple of things to bear in mind.

Firstly, if you think about what you already enjoy in school, you might want to carry that on. If you have an ability in a certain subject and do well, it's worth considering.

You may have a future career in mind too, which will require certain grades from you. This'll mean you have less options to choose from in order to meet the requirements for that career, making the decision a slightly easier one.

For those who have felt restricted in their studies so far, Highers offer plenty of choice, so you will always find something right for you.

What can I do after I gain my Scottish Highers?

Scottish Highers are a good pathway into university. But they are great for employment too – Highers are valued by employers, because they show a good level of education.

You can also use them to go on to study an HNC/HND at an FE college, or vocational or work-based qualifications, such as an apprenticeship, a higher apprenticeship, or a degree apprenticeship.

27 July 2020

Choosing A-level subjects: five points to consider

Even if you know which subjects you want to study at A-level, it still pays to do your research.

The subjects you take at A-level can have a major impact on your future direction. So before embarking on two years' hard work it's well worth doing your research. Here's our five-point guide to making your choices.

1. Ability and enjoyment

Thinking about the subjects you are good at, like and enjoy is a useful starting point.

If you enjoy your studies, you are likely to be more motivated. Similarly, having a natural ability in your chosen subjects can increase your chances of success. For this reason you often need a certain grade at GCSE to study a subject at A-level, so you'll need to check what subjects are open to you.

But beware, there can be significant differences from studying subjects at GCSE to A-level. It doesn't always follow that choosing a subject you enjoyed before will be a safe bet. Even if you feel you're on familiar ground, it pays to do your research.

2. New subjects

Your school or college may offer A-levels in subjects that you've not studied before.

If any new subjects appeal to you, it's worth taking some time to find out what's involved to avoid disappointment later.

Keep a balance in mind. Choosing a couple of familiar subjects alongside one new one, for example, can help leave your options open.

If you want to study certain subjects at university, it is not always necessary – or indeed helpful – to have studied them at A-level. This generally applies to new subjects at A-level, such as law or business studies. When it comes to more traditional subjects, however, an A-level in that subject is usually essential for university study.

3. Subject combinations

Some schools or colleges have restrictions on certain subject combinations, so you will need to check your options.

Similarly, some universities discourage students from taking certain combinations of A-level subjects, especially where there may be an overlap in content, such as with business studies and economics.

The issue of subject combinations can be particularly important if you're studying science subjects.

4. Course content, assessment and workload

You may find it helpful to look at your course syllabus, sometimes called the specifications, which sets out course content and requirements.

Find out which exam board your school or college uses for your chosen subject. Both the content of the course (modules or topics) and the way it is marked (ratio of coursework to exams, amount of exams) can vary. Popular A-level exam boards in the UK include AQA and OCR and you can download the relevant syllabus from their websites.

You may also want to think about the likely workload of your choices. Find out what's required in terms of essay writing, independent reading or extended projects. Consider what this may mean in terms of your chosen subjects.

5. Future plans

If you have a particular career in mind, you may need to choose certain A-levels in order to meet entry requirements for degree courses or further study.

If you don't yet have any career ideas, then keeping your options open can be just as important.

Top universities usually require three academic A-levels, not including general studies or critical thinking. The Russell Group, which represents 24 leading UK universities, has produced a guide which sets out how the subjects you study at A-level can determine which degree courses will be open to you in future. Whatever your plans, it's well worth a read. You can also check entry requirements for university courses on UCAS.

Changing your mind

Making decisions about the unknown is difficult. Things often don't turn out how you expect but you can also be surprised in a positive way – modules with the least appeal at the outset can end up being the most enjoyable.

There's no fail-safe solution here. If you do feel you've made the wrong decision after starting your course, speak to your tutor as it's often possible to change subjects.

Getting advice

Speak to your current school teachers, A-level subject teachers, and current course students to get an idea of what the course involves and what's likely to suit you.

Your parents, family and friends can help shape your views. But remember you are the one who will be doing the work, and it's your future, so it's important to be happy with the choices you make.

You can also speak to a careers advisor for help – visit the National Careers Service for contact information.

20 January 2021

Vocational qualifications

What are the differences between A levels and Vocational Qualifications?

Depending on your sixth form/sixth form college you may have the choice to study A levels on their own or alongside Applied General Qualifications e.g BTECs. Further Education Colleges will offer Applied General Qualifications and also the new T Levels.

A Levels are academic and general qualifications and Applied General Qualifications are courses that are about a vocational area and more practical. T Levels are technical qualifications, equivalent to 3 A Levels that combine classroom study and work placements and train you to do a job.

They are:

♦ Equivalent to each other in terms of grading for example an A Level grade A is equivalent to a BTEC Distinction grade.

♦ You can gain UCAS tariff points and progress on to university study with either A Levels, Applied General Qualifications or T Levels.

The differences:

A Levels

♦ Over 300,000 young people chose to do A Levels last year.

♦ You usually take 3 or 4 different A Level subjects [or you can do one or two alongside an Applied General Qualification].

♦ A Levels are general and academic and are a good choice if you want to keep your career options open.

♦ You can choose a subject you enjoyed at GCSE or pick up a new subject such as Law, Economics or Psychology.

♦ Some degrees and universities will only accept specific subjects and grades for entry to certain degree courses at university.

♦ A Levels do not suit everyone. They are usually assessed at the end of two years by final exams, so you need to be good at independent study, revision and exam technique.

UCAS points for vocational qualifications

BTEC National Extended Diploma	UCAS points	BTEC National Diploma	UCAS points	BTEC National Extended Certificate	UCAS points	T Levels	UCAS points
D*D*D*	168	D*D*	112	D*	56	D*	168
D*D*D	160	D*D	104	D	48	D*D*D*	144
D*DD	144	DD	96		40	M	120
DDM	128	DM	80	M	32	Pass (C or above on core)	96
DMM	112*	MM	64	D*D*D*	24	D*D*D* (D or E on core)	72
MMM	96*	MP	48	P	16		
		PP	32				

Applied General Qualifications

Over 200,000 young people chose to study a Level 3 vocational qualification last year.

These qualifications are known as Applied General Qualifications or known by the exam board they take e.g. BTEC or Cambridge Technicals.

There are a wide range of Applied General Qualifications available, from animal care to performing arts and business to graphic design at lots of different levels.

These qualifications offer the underpinning knowledge of a subject, practical skills and relevant work experience. So these courses will suit you if you have an interest in a specific job area eg Health and Social Care.

These subjects can be taken alongside two A Levels at school or as one course equivalent to two or three A Levels at college.

Generally there are less exams and a range of different assessment methods are likely to be used - such as assignments, tests, observations of learner performance, role-play, work-based assessment, production of visual or audio materials and products. These courses tend to suit people who prefer coursework to exams.

Most students progress on to university to study a degree or go on to an apprenticeship after these qualifications.

If you are intending to study at university in the future it is worth checking if your vocational qualification will allow you to access the course that you are interested in studying, as some degree courses have restrictions.

T Levels - new!

The government has introduced a new qualification called T Levels. T Levels are Level 3 technical qualifications that relate to a vocational area. They are equivalent to 3 x A Levels.

♦ New two year Level 3 qualifications - equivalent to 3 x A levels.

♦ Lead to a specific occupation and available in a whole range of different areas from Cyber Security to Wildlife Management.

♦ Designed by professional bodies, employers and universities so that they are relevant and up to date.

♦ Include at least 3 months work experience and opportunity to build transferable skills and knowledge related to the job area.

♦ Progress on to higher level apprenticeships, jobs and university.

Who are they for?

They are for 16 - 19 year olds who want to focus on developing skills and knowledge of a specific occupation or job sector.

Content provided by Careerpilot, a careers website developed by the WVPC group of university partners in the SW of England.

www.careerpilot.org.uk

GCSE and A-level results have seen record grade inflation – here's why that doesn't matter

An Article from *The Conversation*.

THE CONVERSATION

By Helena Gillespie, Professor of Learning and Teaching in Higher Education and Academic Director of Inclusive Education, University of East Anglia

Exam results are upon us. After the 2020 debacle which saw exams cancelled due to COVID and the first set of algorithm-generated results quickly overturned following complaints of unfairness, what teachers and young people really needed in 2021 was confidence in the grading system.

The process for awarding marks was duly announced in March. And this time, as Education Secretary Gavin Williamson has reiterated, for one year only there would be no algorithm. Instead students would receive marks based on teacher estimates.

Now, results day just wouldn't be the same without the perennial discussion of grade inflation, with commentators comparing the proportion of top grades being awarded. In pre-COVID times, this is seen to undermine the value of the qualifications in the long term. In 2021, though, concerns about grade inflation are misplaced, for three reasons.

The method by which grades have been determined this year differs fundamentally from previous years. Further, as we attempt to make an economic and societal recovery from the pandemic, seeing more young people get the grades they need to get into universities and colleges is to be celebrated, as the guarantee of a well-qualified future workforce.

Finally, and most importantly, given the stress and disruption young people have experienced since COVID hit our shores in March 2020, their achievements should be celebrated, not questioned.

Talk of grade inflation inaccurate and unhelpful

In December 2020 Williamson confirmed that, contrary to the first year of the pandemic, exams in England would not be cancelled in 2021. Guidance subsequently issued by the government's office of qualifications and examinations regulation (Ofqual) and the department for education detailed the range of evidence from students that would be used to determine their grades. This included school-based exams, coursework and portfolios.

The guidance specified that this range of work was to be marked against criteria provided by exam boards, and that the marking would then checked by the school, with exam boards carrying out quality-assurance checks on that marking. This is the system schools have followed.

Students have been awarded the grade their work deserves and teacher judgements have been checked for quality. This is called criterion-based assessment because the assessment is based on work meeting criteria.

By contrast, GCSEs and A-levels in previous years, including the first round of results that were retracted in 2020, were norm-referenced: the results were compared to other students. In this system, students' result depends on their ranking within the cohort, rather than their ability to meet the assessment criteria. This aligns this year's A-levels with BTecs, which have always been criterion-referenced.

Each system, of course, has advantages and disadvantages but the outcomes should not be compared. Student marks this year have been awarded under an approach that is different but no less robust.

There is therefore no reason to suggest that they are less valid than in previous years or that there is a long-term problem with grade inflation. As with so many aspects of life during the pandemic, things are just different this year.

Student success is good for everyone

Record levels of success have been reported, with as many as 45% more students getting top A* grades at A-level according to some reports, and a smaller rise in the number of students achieving A*-C grades too.

Given these results, it seems likely many students will be able to take their places at universities and colleges. This is a good thing for the economy, especially when youth unemployment is at such worryingly high levels.

Places on medicine courses have been in particular demand and the government has already had to offer 9,000 extra places for the coming year. Given the pressure our health service is currently under, it is hard to view more medical students as a problem.

Teacher training has also seen strong growth in numbers. It is inspiring that so many young people are choosing to train for careers in public service. In this way, universities and colleges will play a vital role in pandemic recovery by ensuring young people can be successful. This, surely, is a win-win situation?

Young people deserve praise for their achievements

Despite the best efforts of teachers, schools and support groups, there have been many barriers to success for the class of 2021. Pupils studying for their BTecs and A-levels this year have been uniquely disadvantaged. They have done at least seven of the 20 months of their two-year courses online during lockdown.

Often in their bedrooms and at kitchen tables, away from their usual support network, many found this strange and isolating during what is a crucial period in their education.

Students from disadvantaged backgrounds have been particularly badly affected by this. Some have struggled with poor access to technology and spaces to learn.

Student mental health has been badly affected by the increased isolation, enduring uncertainty and severely restricted access to help during lockdown. We can only hope that this set of circumstances will never be repeated.

It is even more important to celebrate the achievements of young people this week. We need to congratulate them and support them on their way, as the future healthcare workers, teachers and business leaders we will all be depending on for years to come.

10 August 2021

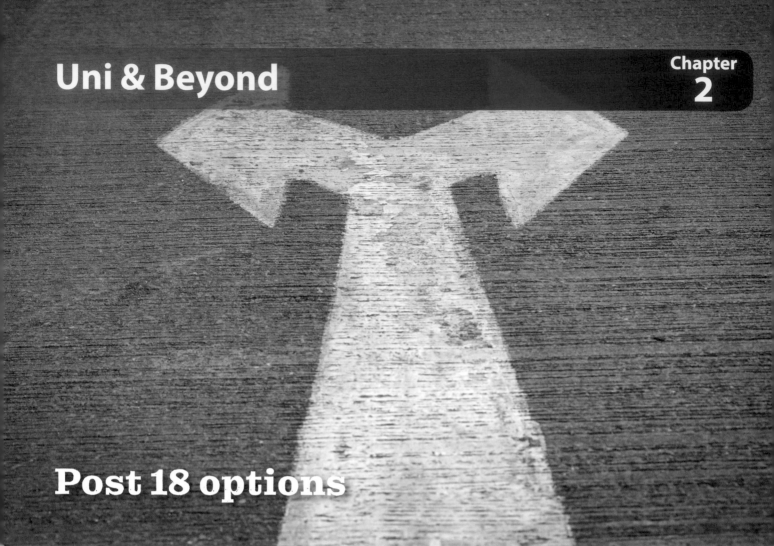

Post 18 options

There are a lot of options to choose from at 18. What's right for you will depend on your situation and the career or job you have in mind.

You may be eligible for the 16 to 19 Bursary Fund, which can help with things like books, travel or equipment if you will struggle with education or training costs.

If you have an Education Health and Care (EHC) plan there may be different and more suitable options available to you.

You can find out about financial support for university from Student Finance.

Combine work and study

Improve your skills and get work experience. Some options allow you to earn while you learn. Spend time in a real workplace while working towards a qualification that employers need.

♦ Traineeships

♦ Supported internships

♦ Apprenticeships

♦ School Leavers Schemes

Continue your studies

You may need to improve your results before taking your next step. You could do a course that gives you time to explore your options or get a work-related qualification.

If you want to move on to a higher level of learning, you could study at a university, college, Institute of Technology (IoT) or a National College. There are opportunities to learn online as well as to study part-time.

♦ Exam retakes

♦ 1 year funded course for ages 18 to 19

♦ Higher technical skills courses

♦ University degree

Get straight into work

Earn a wage, try out a job and start networking. You could even get the skills to start your own business.

♦ Internships

♦ Start a business

♦ Get a kickstart job

♦ Get a job

You may also want to take a gap year before continuing with your studies or getting into work.

Combine work and study

Traineeships

Description: A course that includes a work placement that will get you ready for an apprenticeship or a job. You'll get work experience and some help to apply for your next steps. You can also improve your maths and English skills. You'll get work experience and some help to apply for whatever you do next.

Location: You'll spend a minimum of 70 hours in a work placement with the rest of your time in college or a training centre

Duration: 6 weeks to 1 year

Entry requirements: You need to be aged between 16 to 24 or up to 25 with an Education Health and Care Plan with no higher than a level 3 qualification

Qualifications: English, maths, digital and work-related qualifications

Leads to: Apprenticeship, further education, work

Find out more:

♦ ask your local college or training provider

♦ speak to your school careers adviser

♦ speak to your Jobcentre Plus adviser if you receive benefits

Supported internships

Description: Supported internships are for young people with learning difficulties or learning disabilities, who need extra support to get a job.

Location: You'll spend most of your time on placements with an employer, learning skills for work. You'll also get help from a tutor and a job coach in college or with a specialist provider.

Duration: A minimum of 6 months

Entry requirements: Aged 16-24 with an Education Health and Care Plan

Qualifications: GCSE English and maths

Leads to: Work, traineeship, apprenticeship

Find out more:

♦ from your school or local college

♦ speak to your social worker or a transition worker

♦ speak to your Jobcentre Plus adviser

Apprenticeships

Description: Intermediate, advanced higher and degree apprenticeships combine practical on-the-job skills training with off-the-job learning. You'll get training that is relevant to your job and be paid a salary. Start at a level to suit you, with support if you have special needs or a disability.

Location: You'll spend 80% of your time in the workplace and 20% off-the-job with some study in a college, training centre or Institute of Technology (IoT)

Duration: A minimum of 1 year

Entry requirements: Will be dependent on the industry, job role and apprenticeship level

Qualifications: apprenticeship certificate, diploma, degree and masters depending on level

Leads to: Work, next level of apprenticeship, further education, higher education

Find out more: Visit Gov.uk for more information about Apprenticeships

School leaver schemes

Description: A chance to learn and train with a large company while earning a wage. Offered in sectors like accountancy, engineering, finance, IT, law, leisure and retail. Similar to graduate employment schemes run over a longer period of time.

Location: You'll often rotate between different locations with the same company to get experience and it can include distance learning or time in college or university

Duration: 3 to 7 years

Entry requirements: Usually high grade A levels or equivalent and a keen interest in the sector you want to work in

Qualifications: A university degree and/or professional qualification

Leads to: Professional employment

Find out more: Directly from company websites

Continue your studies

Exam retakes

Description: If you didn't get the results you wanted, you can resit some of your courses or sign up for some new qualifications.

Location: School sixth form, sixth form college or further education college

Duration: 1 year

Entry requirements: 16+

Qualifications: Level 2 and 3 qualifications like GCSE, A level and BTEC

Leads to: Higher level or degree apprenticeship, further education, higher education, work

Find out more: Speak to your school or college careers leader or careers adviser or our careers advisers

1 year funded course for ages 18 to 19

Description: If you can't access work or work-based training in September 2020, you can take a free course to gain work related or technical skills needed by employers. Subjects include engineering, construction, health and social care, and ICT. You can also resit maths and English GCSE if you do not already have a grade 4 or above.

Location: With a college or training provider

Duration: Up to 1 year

Entry requirements: Age 18-19

Qualifications: Level 2 and 3 high value qualifications needed for specific employment sectors

Leads to: Work, higher level or degree apprenticeship

Find out more: By calling the National Career Service advisers or speaking to your local provider

Higher technical skills courses

Description: Learn the higher level skills that employers want in sectors like finance, engineering, management and scientific jobs on a classroom-taught course.

Location: College or university, some of which specialise in subjects as part of an Institute of Technology or National College

Duration: 1 to 2 years

Entry requirements: Varies by course

Qualifications: Higher Nationals (HNC/Ds), foundation degrees, certificate/diploma of higher education and various other technical qualifications

Leads to: Skilled employment in higher technical job or higher levels of study

Find out more: By calling the National Career Service advisers or speaking to your local provider

University degree

Description: An academic course that's usually studied at a higher education institution. Learn through lectures, seminars, group projects and independent study. There's funding available to support you and you can study full or part-time.

Location: At a university, college or online. You could go away to study, stay local or go abroad

Duration: 3 to 4 years

Entry requirements: Universities set their own entry requirements. You'll usually need A Levels or equivalent qualifications

Qualifications: Ordinary or honours degree

Leads to: Postgraduate taught or research degrees, professional qualifications, graduate employment

Find out more: Have a look at the UCAS website to see information about undergraduate degrees

Get straight into work

Internships

Description: A period of work experience where you can try out a job and get to know an industry.

Location: Workplace

Duration: 1 week to 1 year

Entry requirements: Age 16+

Qualifications: N/A

Leads to: Work, university/college, traineeships, apprenticeship

Start a business

Description: Becoming an entrepreneur can be exciting, but think carefully about your ideas and make a solid business plan.

Location: Likely to start at home or shared office

Duration: N/A

Entry requirements: You may need special skills, qualifications or experience before you can start a business. There may also be start-up costs

Qualifications: N/A

Leads to: Work

Get a kickstart job

Description: Get a 6 month paid Kickstart job with a local employer funded by the Government.

Location: Workplace or from home

Duration: 6 months

Entry requirements: Must be aged 16 to 24, in receipt of Universal Credit and at risk of long term unemployment

Qualifications: N/A

Leads to: A stronger CV and better chance of securing your next job

Find out more: Talk to your Universal Credit Work Coach or check the jobhelp site

Get a job

Description: Get straight into the working world to start earning. You'll need an up-to-date CV and cover letter.

Location: Workplace or from home

Duration: Dependent on job offer

Entry requirements: Requirements differ between employers. You may need qualifications or experience for some jobs

Qualifications: N/A

Leads to: Work

Eight questions to help decide if university is your next step

Deciding what to do after A-levels can be a tough decision at any time but this year there are even more things to think about. Here's our guide to finding your way.

1. What's your end goal?

Perhaps not the most obvious starting point, but if you go to university what would you like to do when you finish? Understanding your end goal can help you explore other options and work out if university is your best route.

Knowing what you want is not essential – some people choose university as their next step because they don't have any career ideas but really enjoy a particular subject and want to see where it might take them. Whichever route you choose, being clear about your motivation will help you get the most from your experience.

2. What are the alternatives?

If you don't go to university, what else could you do?

Some options include:

♦ **Higher and Degree Apprenticeships** – these now provide pathways to many careers traditionally followed by graduates.

♦ **Getting a job** – there are lots of opportunities and trainee positions for school leavers. Some people choose to work first and go to university a few years later when they have a better idea of what they really want; others find their feet at work and never look back.

♦ **Taking a Gap Year** – doing something different is a great way to try new things and find out what you like, and may help you make more focused choices.

3. Do you need a degree?

Sometimes, a degree is little more than a passport; employers simply want to know you have one but don't have any real interest in what you've studied. For certain careers, a degree is not necessary and work experience is considered more important. And in other careers, such as medicine, a degree in a set subject is essential.

If you've a specific career idea in mind, there may be different ways you can qualify. For example, did you know you can become a lawyer without going to university? Alternative routes are not always considered a direct equal to a degree – they may only allow to you progress to a certain level in your career – so be sure to check out any limitations they may include.

4. How much will going to university cost?

Fees and talk of future debt and earnings can soon start to seem like Monopoly money and without an idea about your future expenses and living costs, are not always particularly meaningful. That said, it does pay to find out exactly what going to university is likely to cost, what help you can get and what student loans mean. Explore different scenarios – what would student loan repayments look like if you went on to a well-paid, average, or low-paid job? You may not know what you'll end up doing but at least you'll be making a decision with your eyes open.

5. Have you done your research?

Look closely at course content. Just as there is a difference between subjects at GCSE and A-level, so the jump from A-level to degree can bring a different focus. And that's not forgetting subjects you can start from scratch. The Open University's Open Learn offers free university-level modules in a wide range of subjects and can give you a taster of what a full course may involve.

Open days (and virtual open days) can help you get a feel for what you like, both in terms of courses and the wider university experience.

Consider employment prospects for your chosen course – where have recent graduates ended up?

6. What about additional benefits?

As with many aspects of life, the biggest advantages of any chosen path are often the unexpected ones. In the long term, people reflecting on their university days often find the wider benefits, such as developing confidence, making connections, or involvement with clubs and societies, more important than their actual studies. These things can all be gained in other ways – and no one would suggest going to university just because you're likely to make some great friends or write for the student paper – but what you end up valuing the most may have little to do with your course.

7. Can you do things differently?

Going to university doesn't have to mean you need to follow the standard route of moving to a new town and becoming a full-time student – there are different and more flexible ways to get a degree which may suit you better. You could:

♦ Study at your local university and live at home.

♦ Do a part-time degree that you can combine with work or other commitments.

♦ Study with the Open University (distance learning courses which mean you can study at a time and place that suits you).

♦ Do a sponsored degree. Certain employers will pay for you to do your degree but you may need to work for them first and/or for a certain period after you graduate.

8. What's right for you?

It can be easy to fall into doing the same as your friends or what your parents or teachers expect so it's important to consider if your next step is really right for you.

It's also worth bearing in mind that people looking back at their university days sometimes do so with rose-tinted glasses – they may have gone to university when fees were much lower or before they were introduced, or graduated when a degree was a sure-fire route to a good job.

One thing is certain, advancements in technology and the changing nature of the job market means that many jobs of the future don't yet exist. The ability to continue learning – whatever route you take – is set to become an essential skill in working life.

Top takeaway: You can't know how your life will turn out if you go to university or if you choose a different route, but you can find out the facts and consider the alternatives.

How to choose a university and the right degree

Before applying to uni, there are some big choices to make. What's the best degree for you? How do you find the right university? This guide will make your decisions a whole lot easier.

By Jake Butler

If you've already started thinking about university, you'll have probably been told by a lot of people that it will be the best few years of your life. We think they're right.

At uni, you get to be independent, meet loads of new people and just generally have an amazing time. Oh, and you can learn a few things while you're there, too.

But, we do know that the period leading up to uni can also feel pretty daunting at times. In this guide, we'll talk you through how to find your ideal university and degree. We want you to arrive at uni for freshers' week and know it's the right place for you.

How to choose a university course

Here are the best ways to find a degree that's perfect for you:

Research your degree options online

While some people know straight away which course they want to study, for most of us, finding the right degree will be a bit trickier.

Maybe you're interested in more than one career after uni, or there might be a few different degrees that have caught your eye. Either way, researching your options online is a great place to start.

Take a look at the UCAS subject guides – they have handy info about the general entry requirements and desirable A Levels or Scottish Highers for each degree. And check out our list of unusual university degrees too – it may inspire you to do a slightly less conventional course.

Consider doing a degree that's different to your A Levels

It's worth thinking about whether you'd like to do any of the subjects you're studying at A Level (or equivalent) as a degree. It will help you know whether you'll enjoy a subject at university if you're already studying it to a pretty high level.

Plus, your online research will give you a good idea of which other degrees are open to you based on your A Level or Higher subjects.

But remember: you don't necessarily need to have studied a degree at A Level to do a degree in it. Think about your specific skills and knowledge – what are you gaining from each of your current subjects that could help you in a degree?

If you'd like to venture out into something completely different, it's well worth looking into whether you could still apply with the A Levels you have taken.

And, if you're unsure whether you would be accepted onto a degree with your A Levels, we recommend chatting to teachers and reaching out to universities directly to find out.

Ask teachers, friends and family for advice

Firstly, talk to teachers about your options – they'll know which degrees are available to you based on your A Level or Higher subjects and predicted grades. And, from knowing you, they should be able to identify a degree you'd do well in.

It's then a good idea to get advice from friends and family. Again, they'll know you well and they might even draw attention to some of your skills that you haven't yet thought of exploring in a degree.

Also, if you know of any professionals working in your goal industry – perhaps family, friends or people you've come across on social media – you could reach out to them and ask for some advice.

If you can, find out what they studied and how they've got to where they are now to get a good idea of what route would be best for you to take.

Narrow down degree options until you find the right one

Once you know your options, take a gander at course syllabuses to find out which topics you'd be studying in each degree and how you'd be assessed (i.e. are the courses essay-based or practical?).

And, after you've narrowed down possible degrees to a choice of one or two, attend as many university open days and taster days as you can – seeing example lectures and chatting to uni staff will help you know whether a degree's right for you.

Also, if you're choosing a degree with a particular career in mind, start doing work experience in that industry and, while on placements, ask for advice from your managers about what and where you could study.

How to choose a university

These are the most effective ways to find the right university for you:

Write a list of all universities you're interested in

There are over 160(!) universities in the UK – whittling your choices down to five is not easy.

The key is to be selective about which universities to pick. What are your predicted grades? If you find out which unis ask for these grades as entry requirements, you've got yourself a pretty good list of options to start with.

After you've made this list, find out as much about each one as possible. Order their prospectuses, attend open days and, if possible, talk to people who have been there.

If you know any family, friends or even friends-of-friends who went to a university on your list, ask them about what it's really like to go there.

Think about the location of universities

Once you've found a few unis you like the look of, you should think about their location. Whether you're planning to move away for your degree or commute from home, the location matters.

On open days, think about how you feel about the campus and uni buildings. You will be spending a lot of time here during your degree, so it's hugely important that you feel comfortable and happy.

It's also a good idea to spend some time wandering around the local town or city centre. Have a look at the shops and bars, find the local tourist attractions and ask yourself if you'd like to live there for three years. If the answer's yes, you'll know you've found one of your five choices!

Be realistic with target grades

When unis look at your application, they'll want to know if you can achieve the grades they're asking for.

It's a good idea to apply for three places that ask for similar grades to the ones you're predicted.

Then, you can choose one with slightly higher entry requirements as a goal, and one with lower requirements as a back-up choice. That way, you've got an even better chance of getting snapped up.

Which universities offer the best student lifestyle?

Everyone has a different idea about what makes the ideal student lifestyle.

If you're hoping for great nightlife at uni, check out the best (and worst) places for uni nightlife.

Also, have a look online for the local student club nights. When you see loads of clubs boasting weekly events for students, this is a very good sign. And, if you're shown around the campus by students on open days, have a chat with them about the nightlife – they're the experts, after all.

For sporty students, think about the sports societies and facilities on offer. Some places might be particularly geared up for your favourite sport, so it's worth looking into. For example, Loughborough University has a great reputation for its world-class sports facilities.

Students who are more into the arts can look for unis with art, music and theatre to see (and do) on campus. Maybe have a look at the Barber Institute of Fine Arts at the University of Birmingham if you're interested in art, or the Cambridge Footlights if you're craving time on stage – there are so many options out there.

Whatever your interests, if you want to go to uni, there will be one for you.

Alternatives to university

Although uni can be great if it's what you really want, the truth is that it's not for everyone – and that's okay.

You should never feel like you have to go to uni just because your friends are going, or you feel it's expected of you – there are so many other routes you could take. If your gut's saying that uni's not for you, it's a good idea to listen.

Our guide to the alternatives to university has everything you need to know about your other options, like taking a higher apprenticeship or starting a business.

5 May 2021

How to write a personal statement for university

Writing a personal statement for university is up there as one of the most dreaded stages of applying to uni. But, worry not – this guide will help you write an application to be proud of.

By Laura Brown

Once you've chosen your degree and shortlisted your five dream unis, you might feel like a lot of the hard work's done. But, alas, there's still the teeny tiny matter of a personal statement – every uni applicant's favourite task...

You've got 47 lines (or 4,000 characters) to 'sell' yourself to your chosen universities. And, with these tips, you'll be able to write a UCAS personal statement that impresses unis from start to finish.

10 best ways to write a UCAS personal statement

These are the best ways to write a stand-out personal statement as a university applicant:

1. Start the personal statement with a powerful introduction

To stand out and impress universities, the best way to start your personal statement is to say something surprising and memorable.

Do you know how many times uni admissions staff will read 'I've always wanted to be an [insert job role here]'? Too many.

Maybe think about the exact moment you decided to study your degree, or a fact which absolutely fascinates you about the subject.

Don't just say it's 'what you want to do' – show it from the first line.

2. Be creative with your language

We're not suggesting you recite a thesaurus and write about your substantial and unremitting desideratum to meditate on your field of reference. Because really, please don't.

Instead, just be wary that some words and phrases are very overused in UCAS applications. Avoiding these terms is a subtle yet effective way of standing out.

Common words and phrases to avoid in university personal statements

♦ 'Passionate' – Please trust us on this one. We hope you are very passionate about your chosen subject, but there'll be a dizzying number of other applicants repeatedly using the same word. By providing the many reasons why you're passionate, your enthusiasm will be clear without you having to explicitly say it.

♦ 'Like' – Telling an admissions officer you would 'like' to study a degree is like saying their course looks 'nice' (which should also be avoided FYI). If you know from doing research and attending open days that you'd love to study your chosen subject, don't be shy in saying so.

♦ 'I couldn't put into words...' – We know it can be hard to explain why you chose a course, but the whole purpose of a personal statement is for you to put all of your excitement and ideas into words – there's no point telling unis that you can't do exactly that. If you're struggling,

have a chat with a friend or family member about your reasons for applying. This will help clarify your main points.

♦ 'Firstly'/'Secondly'/'Finally' – Starting each paragraph like this will make your uni personal statement sound really rigid and unimaginative. They're not necessary, so we'd suggest taking out these words and using those all-important characters elsewhere.

3. Refer to extra reading

If you've read an academic book or essay related to your chosen degree which you were struck by, we'd definitely recommend writing a few lines about it.

You don't need to say too much when you're writing a personal statement for university, but adding a little bit about why you found it particularly interesting/surprising/controversial will give unis an insight into how you think.

This is a particularly effective technique if the subject you're applying for isn't one you're currently studying at sixth form/college – it shows you've done your research, care about the subject and (importantly!) you're the kind of student who puts in extra work to learn.

4. Avoid quotes and clichés

4,000 characters (roughly 500 words) might sound like a lot, but each one is precious in a personal statement. Any characters spent quoting other people or using unoriginal phrases are ones that could have been used to explain why unis should offer you a place.

So, maybe forget the quotes you've found on Google from Einstein or J.K. Rowling – say something which reflects *you*, not them.

5. Link every point you make to your chosen subject

Whatever you mention in your personal statement, make sure you back it up with reasons why it will help you in your degree.

For example, when talking about your A Levels, write about what you've learnt from each subject and how it will help you in your degree. Even if you think a subject's not relevant, it'll still be teaching you tonnes of new skills which are bound to come in handy.

Or, if you have a relevant hobby, explain how it's helped you develop as a student – consider whether you're more determined from competing in sports, or you've got great concentration from learning instruments, or you burst with confidence when performing on stage. Unis will want to know.

6. Be concise

If you start waffling to fill out the 4,000 characters, unis will notice. You want your personal statement to be filled with loads of interesting points which present you as a well-rounded and capable applicant, and the best way to do this is to write concisely.

Again, back up every point and explain why it's relevant, but do so in as few words as possible to leave room for all of the other reasons universities must offer you a place.

This is especially important if you find that 4,000 characters is too little a space for you to describe yourself. It can be done, you just need to work on your wording.

7. Write a confident ending to your personal statement

Just as you need a good personal statement introduction, it's super important to make an impact with your ending.

You should aim to make a lasting impression and finish it on a positive note. One of the best ways to do this is by rounding off your application with a confident (but not arrogant) assertion that, based on everything you've told them, you're sure your chosen degree is perfect for you.

8. Carefully plan your personal statement's structure

Particularly if you have loads of things you want to include in your personal statement, it's vital that your points flow seamlessly from one to the next.

When first thinking about the structure, you could draft a list of all the reasons you're choosing this degree. You can then rank each point from most significant to least and, the higher the ranking, the sooner it should be mentioned in the personal statement.

If you're struggling to decide on the best structure for your uni personal statement, try following these general guidelines:

♦ Beginning – Start by focussing on your personal reasons for choosing the degree, giving an overview of why it's perfect for you based on your experience, interests and skills.

♦ Middle – Explain how your A Levels will help you with your chosen degree and discuss any important school achievements (e.g. leadership positions, contributions to clubs, campaigns you've been involved in, and so on).

♦ End – Discuss your hobbies towards the end to show you're well-rounded with lots of interests and talents. Just keep in mind that, even if these points feel less relevant, you'll still need to explain how they will help you as a uni student by developing particular skills and qualities.

9. Write several drafts of your personal statement

You'll need to be prepared for a pretty long cycle of reading, editing and re-reading your personal statement until you're ready to submit it – but it's so, so worth it (honestly). The more time and effort you put into it, the better it will be.

Don't worry about making the first draft perfect. Focus on writing the bulk of the content initially and then, gradually, you can start tweaking, developing and refining it until you've written the best possible UCAS personal statement.

10. Ask others to read through your UCAS application

After spending hours writing up the first draft of your personal statement, it can be hard when others suggest ways to change it – but this kind of feedback is incredibly important.

Remember that your friends, parents and teachers are looking at it through fresh eyes – as admissions staff will too – so ask for honest feedback and try to take their suggested changes on board.

How to write a personal statement for multiple courses

If you're writing a personal statement for two subjects that have a lot in common (e.g. English Literature and Creative Writing, or Medicine and Biomedicine), it should be quite easy to talk generally about them both, as long as you focus on the overlapping parts of each subject.

But, it can be a bit more tricky to apply for two completely unrelated subjects, either as a joint degree or at different unis.

In this case, it's worth dedicating parts of your UCAS personal statement to each subject.

Try to refer to skills and work experience throughout the application which would be useful for either degree. This way, you can make sure unis will be reading relevant info the whole time, even when you're writing about a different subject.

What to avoid in a university personal statement

To write the best possible personal statement for uni, avoid these mistakes:

♦ Bunched up paragraphs – You should aim to add a line space between each paragraph so that it's easier to read and looks neater. Each line space will use up a character, but it'll be worth it.

♦ Starting every sentence with 'I' – Try to add a bit of variety to the application. Most sentences starting with 'I' can usually be reordered in some way.

♦ Changing your writing style – While it's important to avoid grammatical/spelling errors and come across positively, it's not ideal to sound pretentious or write in a tone that doesn't feel natural to you.

♦ Repeating yourself – There's no need to go over information that's already on your UCAS form, like predicted grades. All this does is eat up some valuable characters and leave you less space to explain how great you are.

♦ Overdoing jokes – Some subtle wit can be effective if done well, but don't try too hard to make your personal statement funny. That's not what unis are looking for.

♦ Plagiarism – This should really go without saying, but never copy anything from other examples you've seen online or at school. Your personal statement has to be original, or else unis will see through it.

17 September 2021

Should I go to university or do an apprenticeship in the UK?

By Chloe Lane

Once you've completed your sixth-form education, you may be unsure which path to take next. If this is you, there's really no reason to panic – there are plenty of options available to you.

Whether you choose to attend university or decide to go down the apprenticeship route, both options can give you the opportunity to complete a full bachelor's degree. Degree apprenticeships will allow you to gain a degree whilst learning about your industry with on-the-job training.

Attending university and pursuing an apprenticeship both come with their own sets of pros and cons so it's really up to you to decide which option is best given your own personal circumstances.

We spoke to a couple of apprentices about their experiences: Stephanie Hayes, who started her cyber security technologist apprenticeship with QA in 2017, and Elena King who is currently pursuing a solicitor apprenticeship in a UK law firm. We also spoke to Adam Snook, a third year history and international relations student at the University of Reading.

Read on as we compare the two options so you can decide which path is right for you…

Will it limit my options in the future?

University

If you decide to attend university, you'll have the opportunity to study a wide range of subjects, although admission to some courses may be dependent on the subjects studied at A-level.

'I didn't know what I wanted to do for a career, so university gave me a wider range of options', says Adam Snook, a third-year history and international relations student at the University of Reading.

University degrees give you some time to figure out what you want to do for your future career, whilst studying a subject of your choice in depth and allowing you to gain a variety of transferable skills, which'll be useful in a wide range of industries.

Apprenticeship

If you decide to study an apprenticeship you will be studying while you work in your chosen field. The downside of this is that your options are likely to be slightly more limited in the future, as you will have specialized in a career path quite early on.

Despite this, there are an increasing number of options for apprenticeships in fields like business, accounting, engineering, IT, education, retail and media. Degree apprenticeships will allow you to earn a degree in your desired industry, whilst pursuing on the job training.

Elena King started on an admin apprenticeship in a law firm, but soon found that this is not what she enjoyed. 'I wanted to do more than admin', she told TU.

However, her apprenticeship helped her find a career that suited her; 'when I changed teams, I was offered much more legal work and I was eventually pretty much working as a paralegal/trainee'. She adds 'When I saw the solicitor apprenticeships available, I went for it.'

What qualifications will I earn?

University

At university, you will earn your bachelor's degree, master's degree or PhD, depending on which level you study at.

Apprenticeship

The qualifications you earn in your apprenticeship really depend on the type of apprenticeship you decide to pursue. The different types of apprenticeship include:

◆ Intermediate - equivalent to five good GCSE passes.

◆ Advanced - equivalent to two A-level passes.

◆ Higher - equivalent to the first stages of higher education, such as a foundation degree.

◆ Degree - equivalent to a bachelor's or master's degree.

'I took the Level 4 Cyber Security Technologist apprenticeship – a higher apprenticeship from QA based around the skills required for upcoming cybersecurity professionals' says Stephanie Haynes, who started her apprenticeship at QA. 'By completing the QA apprenticeship, I am now a fully-fledged cyber security analyst'.

How much will they cost?

University

In England, an undergraduate university degree will cost you a maximum of £9,250 per year. In Scotland you will not be charged if you are from Scotland, or the EU, although students from England, Wales or Northern Ireland will be expected to pay up to £9,250.

In Wales, you will be charged up to £9,000 for home students and £3,925 for EU and Northern Irish students. Students in Northern Ireland will be charged up to £4,030 for home students and £9,250 for students from elsewhere in the UK.

Stephanie spoke of her difficulty finding a university degree program that suited her fiscal needs; 'all of the degrees available to me at the time were full-time, campus based degrees which would have made it difficult for me to support myself and complete a degree at the same time'.

Apprenticeship

One advantage of undertaking an apprenticeship over a university education is that you will be earning money while studying.

In the UK, if you are under 19, this will be £3.90 per hour minimum. If you're over 19, this will be the National Minimum Wage (at the time of writing this is £6.15 for 18 to 20-year olds, £7.70 for 21 to 24-year olds, and £8.21 for 25 and over).

If you're doing a degree apprenticeship, the cost of your course will be divided amongst the course providers and the government, meaning that you will complete your degree and be completely debt free. However, this means that degree apprentices don't qualify for student loans.

Elena revealed that this was one aspect that really appealed to her about apprenticeships; 'I really like that I won't be in debt at the end'.

What is the lifestyle like?

University

At university you will either be studying full time or part time and may be living at home, in private accommodation or in university halls. If you're a full-time student in the UK, you will have three terms, running from September to October, to around May, with time off for Easter, Christmas and summer.

'University life can be whatever you want it to be. You can get involved with whatever you're interested in and you can choose when you want to work. Some people treat it like a nine to five job and others just go when it suits them,' says Adam.

'I think that attending university has its own unique experiences in the same way that completing an apprenticeship does. Before I started [the apprenticeship], I did consider the social aspect – uni seems to be a great place to socialize and network', says Stephanie.

Apprenticeship

In an apprenticeship you will combine working with studying; learning job specific skills, working with experienced staff and studying at a college or training organization to gain specific qualifications.

'80 percent of my time would be spent working on the projects assigned to me in my job, and the other 20 percent was either spent away from work attending classroom training, or putting a bit of time aside at work to focus on my apprenticeship studies,' says Stephanie

The apprenticeship experience will differ depending on the company you're working for, the location and the type of apprenticeship you are undertaking.

Apprentices are also entitled to 21 days paid holiday plus bank holidays in the UK.

How long will they take to complete?

Universities

Your undergraduate university degree will take two to four years to complete if you're a full-time student. This will depend on your course and where you decide to study. The most common length of a master's degree is a year, and a PhD takes around three to four years to complete in the UK.

Apprenticeship

Apprenticeships will take between one to six years, depending on the type of apprenticeship you are pursuing. You may then be offered a full-time position with the company.

15 March 2021

Five reasons why you should consider choosing an apprenticeship

Apprenticeships are a brilliant option for people of all ages to launch their careers in a huge range of exciting industries or upskill at various levels.

There are thousands of apprenticeship vacancies on offer, with more than 640 high-quality apprenticeships approved for use by employers – meaning someone could pursue a career as anything from a space engineering technician to a junior advertising creative.

Here's five reasons why you should consider choosing an apprenticeship.

1. It's a paid job

Apprenticeships are an exciting option for anyone wanting to gain high quality training in their chosen field because they offer you the chance to 'earn while you learn'.

An apprenticeship is a paid job where you can learn and gain valuable workplace experience.

Alongside your on-the-job training, as an apprentice you will spend at least 20% of your time in off-the-job training with a training provider, such as a college or university, learning the skills you need to become occupationally competent.

2. You get high quality training

Apprenticeships help people to develop the necessary skills and experience to succeed in their chosen career.

Breaking it down, an apprenticeship includes:

◆ paid employment with holiday leave

◆ hands-on-experience in a sector/role of interest

◆ at least 20% off-the-job training

◆ formal assessment which leads to a nationally recognised qualification

Off-the-job training is delivered by subject experts and can include teaching theory, such as classroom lessons, lectures, online learning; practical training, such as shadowing, mentoring, industry visits; learning support; and time to write assignments.

All of this combines to provide high quality training for people to progress in their chosen sector.

3. The wide range of choices on offer

There have never been so many great apprenticeship options available in such a diverse range of sectors at multiple levels, going right up to degree level.

There are now 642 approved apprenticeships all developed working closely with leading employers so that apprentices gain the specific skills and knowledge that they need to do the job and start rewarding careers.

There's something for everyone – from school leavers to those looking to upskill in their careers, and those seeking a career change.

Hayley Spencer is a Graduate Engineering Apprentice and Mentor with Princess Yachts, which has been hiring apprentices since 1997.

She completed a four-year engineering scheme with Princess and is now mentoring first year apprentices – passing on the knowledge and experience she has gained with the company.

4. It's rewarding

Apprenticeships can unlock doors for people, and they can be lucrative. Many world-class careers have been built on a solid apprenticeship.

What you earn will depend on the location, industry and type of apprenticeship you choose.

At a minimum, if you're aged 16 to 18 or in the first year of your apprenticeship, you're entitled to the apprentice rate. If you're 19 or over and have completed the first year of your apprenticeship, you're entitled to the National Minimum Wage.

But many employers pay a lot more and offer their apprentices a competitive salary.

The good news is that 91% of apprentices go on to secure employment or go on to further study after completing their training. In terms of earning potential, for all levels of learning in apprenticeships, earnings rise five years after study, figures for those who achieved apprenticeships in 2018/19 show.

And to give an example, one year after study, the data shows the highest earnings for those who achieved an advanced apprenticeship that year were in Engineering (£31,090), Public Services (£29,390) and Manufacturing Technologies (£29,150).

Beyond earnings, there are a range of other rewards for taking on an apprenticeship.

Learning 'on the job' means networking opportunities, ongoing support from the employer, peer-to-peer support, paid annual leave.

5. More and more young people are considering an apprenticeship

And finally, you'll be joining an increasing number of young people who are considering an apprenticeship as their next step.

Some 342,000 people out of the 750,000 who have set up their UCAS account in the last six months say they are interested in an apprenticeship, according to John Cope, director of strategy, policy and public affairs at UCAS.

This is up 123% on the previous year. Searches for apprenticeships on UCAS.com also reached 2 million this year, up 45% on the previous year.

It comes after research released by UCAS in August 2021 suggested that more than three quarters (78%) of students who received their A level or Level 3 vocational and technical results last summer, but did not plan to immediately start a three year full-time undergraduate degree, were interested in starting an apprenticeship.

The research showed that 56% of 17-19-year-olds, who were not intending to start a traditional degree course in the autumn, considered an apprenticeship.

A further 22% said their main plan was an apprenticeship (16% higher/degree level, 6% advanced level).

7 February 2022

Coping with exam stress

Both exams and the anticipation of results can be a stressful time. The Mix gives you some tips for getting through it.

By Holly Turner

Why am I so stressed by exams?

Exam stress could be caused by:

♦ Pressure from parents and relatives to do well

♦ The need to get high grades to get on track for the career you really want

♦ Uncertainty about what to do next – 'There are so many options, what if I make the wrong choice?'

♦ The feeling of everything changing in your life – you have moved away to university or going to new college for example.

These fears and concerns are completely natural – your mates are probably feeling exactly the same, whether they let on or not. If these anxieties start to overwhelm you, don't worry – there are things you can do to help look after your mental health.

What is stress?

Stress is the reaction people have to excessive demands or pressures. It's very common to feel stressed around exam time. You might feel there's a huge amount of pressure to do well, or anxious you can't fit all the revision in. The build-up to results day can also leave you feeling overwhelmed and run down. Read our guide to understanding stress.

Not only does stress mess with your mind – in extreme cases it can affect your physical health. Stressed out people have higher blood pressure. They are also prone to heart disease, colitis (inflammation of the bowels), thyroid disorders, and ulcers. But don't worry – it's extremely rare for stress to get so far out of control, especially if you deal with it when the first symptoms appear.

What are the symptoms of exam stress?

♦ Difficulty getting to sleep or difficulty waking up in the morning

♦ Constant fatigue

♦ Forgetfulness

♦ Aches and pains for no apparent reason

♦ Poor appetite

♦ Social withdrawal

♦ Loss of interest in activities

♦ Increased anxiety and irritability

♦ 'Flying off the handle'

♦ Increased heart rate

♦ Migraines/headaches

♦ Blurred vision

♦ Dizziness

Everyone has bad days, but if you've noticed three or more of the above symptoms and you've experienced them for some weeks you may need to do something about your stress levels. Visit your doctor (GP) to rule out other possible reasons for the symptoms such as depression. If you are stressed, your GP may be able to advise you.

How can I deal with exam stress?

If you are suffering from stress, try some of the following ways to calm down and relax:

♦ Try to make time for yourself away from your studies to wind down. For example, relaxing in a warm bubble bath, listening to soothing music and shutting out the world for a while.

♦ Take time for your mind and body to relax. Chatting with friends, meditation, yoga or just watching a bit of telly can take the edge off.

♦ Take time to exercise. Regular and frequent exercise is a good stress reducer.

♦ Eat well – skipping meals will deplete your energy and leave you drained.

♦ Talk to your family and friends. Making time to see your mates will help you unwind and let you unburden any problems.

25 May 2021

Anxiety UK's top tips for managing exam stress

Exam season can be a daunting and worrying time for many students and can lead to increased anxiety and stress, especially if you have never been through the experience of sitting formal exams before. Here at Anxiety UK, we would like to share our top tips for managing stress and anxiety to help you manage your worries and focus on getting the best results you can!

Organise your revision

Try to take a little extra time to organise a revision schedule. This allows you to plan your time and make sure you can look at every subject comprehensively before your exams. If you stick to your plan as much as possible you can be confident you have spent enough time on all of your subjects and you are well prepared. Preparation is certainly key.

Get a good night's sleep

It may seem like a good idea to stay up late and cram in some extra revision the night before an exam but, getting a good night's sleep is really important and will ensure that you are well rested and prepared to sit your exam the following day. Sleep is really important for our wellbeing and whilst being stressed can cause sleep problems, lack of sleep can also cause us to feel more stressed.

Eat healthily and keep hydrated

Whilst snacking on treats whilst revising might be a temptation and gives you a big sugar rush, it's important to make sure you are eating healthily to ensure you have plenty of sustained energy and to keep you alert. This can also help you to feel less sluggish and can reduce anxiety. Ensure that you keep yourself well hydrated (take a bottle of water with you to exams) and avoid the temptation to have drinks that are high in caffeine as these types of drink may result in you feeling more anxious and jittery – not what you need when sitting an exam.

Make sure you give yourself plenty of time on the day of the exam

Allow yourself to get ready in plenty of time before your exam(s) and plan your journey in advance. Getting stuck in a traffic jam or missing the bus can cause you to feel stressed and anxious right before your exam and is an unnecessary source of stress to have to cope with. Getting to your exam in good time and ensuring that you have a moment to relax can make sure you feel prepared before going into the exam room. Practising mindfulness can really help you to still your mind before going into an exam – ensuring that you enter the exam room feeling calm and grounded.

Try this exercise to ground yourself:

Find 5 things you can see

Find 4 things you can hear

Find 3 things you can smell

Find 2 things you can touch

Find 1 thing you can taste

Take some time for yourself!

It can be easy to feel guilty when taking a break when in exam season and to feel that you should always be working. However, taking breaks and having 'down time' to do things you enjoy can help you to feel less stressed and overwhelmed by the exams. One way to make sure you feel relaxed is taking 10 minutes to meditate or do a mindfulness exercise. At Anxiety UK we have a partnership with Headspace as part of our membership. With Headspace you can complete 5, 10 or 20 minute mindfulness and meditation sessions that can help you to feel much more relaxed and calm.

Going for a walk and simply going outside can really help with managing stress as can exercising. You will often find that your revision is more productive when you intersperse it with short breaks.

And finally....

If you are still feeling pressure from exam stress, workbooks can be a really useful tool to help manage anxiety as they provide techniques to help overcome the fears surrounding exams.

We recommend the following book in particular:

Starving the Exam Stress Gremlin by Katie Collins-Donnelly

This book is part of the award-winning 'Starving the Gremlin' series and is full of engaging activities. Rooted in Cognitive Behavioural Therapy (CBT), it is packed with strategies to help the reader manage exam stress by changing how they think and act.

For more information please visit our website: https://www.anxietyuk.org.uk/products/children-and-anxiety/starving-the-exam-stress-gremlin/

If however you feel that your anxiety has become difficult to manage, Anxiety UK has lots of support available for you to access. Give our helpline a call and one of our friendly volunteers will be able to talk you through your options (03444 775 774). Alternatively, pop on our website (www.anxietyuk.org.uk) where you can access our live chat, email or text support services.

It's important to remember that this is a time that will pass, along with the stress that you are experiencing, and that you are not alone – help is available if you need it.

Good luck from the Anxiety UK team!

13 May 2019

Don't calm down! Exam stress may not be fun but it can help you get better marks

An article from *The Conversation*.

By Mandie Shean, Lecturer, School of Education, Edith Cowan University

THE CONVERSATION

Two-thirds of young people experience levels of exam stress that mental health organisation ReachOut describes as 'worrying'.

Research shows high levels of exam stress can interfere with attention and reduce working memory, leading to lower performance. Early experiences of anxiety and stress can also set a precedent for mental-health problems in adulthood.

But how we see stress can actually make a difference to the way it affects us. Research shows if we believe stress is a helpful response that will increase our performance in a challenging event, it can be a tool that works to our advantage.

From good stress to bad stress

Stress is a normal experience when we have a challenging event. We can experience stress when learning something new, starting a new job or being in a race.

Our experience of 'stress' is actually our body getting us ready to take on the challenge. A stress response is helpful as it can increase oxygen to the brain and improve attention, focus, energy and determination.

The runner in a race needs to be 'stressed' to compete successfully. The young person sitting in an exam room needs it too.

Studies show people who are clear about their feelings are more likely to thrive on anxiety and stress and possibly use these to achieve their goals and find satisfaction at work.

Stress and anxiety can work for you. But they become bad when we evaluate events as a threat rather than a challenge and when we believe we don't have enough resources to cope.

Exams are often treated as a threat because there is potential harm or loss related to our self-worth, identity, and commitments, goals and dreams. If we fail, we think we are a failure and we may never get the future we had hoped for. Our whole life is at stake.

How do we make stress good?

To put it simply, stress can be good if we believe it's good. It'll work for us if we develop a mind-set that stress helps our performance, health and well-being (rather than seeing it as debilitating).

In a study from the United States, one group of young people were given information about stress before sitting an exam. The reading material explained stress was not harmful, but that it had evolved to help us cope and perform better. Another group were told to just ignore stress and suppress their emotions.

Researchers found the first group performed significantly better in the exam (average five marks improvement) than the group who used the ignore-and-relax approach.

In another study of exam stress, students who saw stress as an opportunity and used it for self-growth had increased performance and decreased emotional exhaustion. But students who saw stress as a threat showed decreased effort and performance.

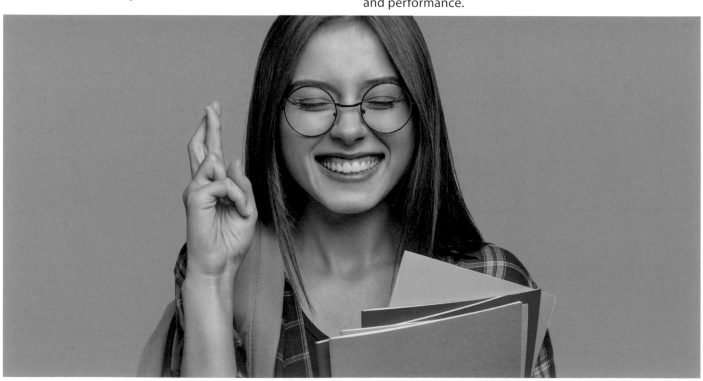

These studies didn't examine how to eliminate exam stress. Instead they examined a change in the way students responded to it. Here are some tips for you use stress to your advantage.

Four ways to make stress work for you

1. Read your body differently

Start to read your stress response as being there to help you prepare for the challenge. Instead of seeing it as a threat, try to see it as a coping tool. When you are experiencing stress, you can say to yourself:

I am feeling a little uncomfortable; my heart is beating faster, but my body is getting me ready to compete.

2. Reframe the meaning of the event

Rather than framing exams as a threat, try to frame them as a challenge. Part of the reason they are seen as a threat is because your whole future, identity and worth appear to be at stake. This is not true. Exams are one very small part of your life that does not decide your whole future.

There are always other options, different pathways and opportunities. Vera Wang failed to get into the Olympic ice-skating team and became a world famous dress designer. Sometimes the path we imagine looks a little different.

Not all journeys are straight, and the best ones can have diversions.

3. Accept stress and negative emotions

Some common ways people approach stress is to try to relax, ignore stress and try to reduce it. These approaches actually reinforce that stress is 'bad' rather than accepting it as a natural and helpful response. These approaches also lead to poorer performance and emotional exhaustion.

Rather than ignoring the emotions, it's better to feel them, accept them, and then try to use them to your advantage. You can say to yourself:

I feel this way because this goal is important to me, and my body is responding this way because it is getting me ready to perform.

4. Add to your resources

Clearly, changing your mind-set is only helpful if you have the resources to cope. It would be like an athlete who is about to compete but has not trained. Put time into study, study in different ways (read, write ideas in your own words, talk about the ideas, draw them) and give yourself time to practise these ideas.

When you have done this, your stress response then draws on these resources.

Stress will always be present in our lives as we take on new challenges and grow as a person. When we see low-level stress as a threat it becomes one. It becomes a red flag that we are not coping, that these feelings are wrong and we should retreat. This is not true.

However, if you are feeling severe stress and anxiety in different settings and for an extended period of time you should see your GP and get support.

15 October 2019

What is the best way to revise?

Experienced tutor Claire Senior, shares her insights into the best way to revise for GCSE and A Level exams, covering everything from past papers to effective revision techniques.

By Claire Senior

If you've just Googled 'best way to revise', then chances are, you're in need of some study motivation and a few pointers to help you prepare for your upcoming exams. As aviation pioneer Amelia Earhart said, 'The most effective way to do it, is to do it.' Having said that...some methods of revision have a much greater impact than others. It's easy to fall into the trap of thinking that you're doing lots of revision because you're spending an hour staring at a book. Fifteen minutes of adopting another method can often be a much more efficient use of time.

So, why do students still fall into the 'sitting in the library is work' thinking trap? Well, because it's easier than the methods that require brain power and analysis. Yet, it's much less effective.

Here are my top tips on the best way to revise, so you'll pass exams with flying colours.

Find out what you'll be tested on

While it might be interesting to read around the subject (and helpful in many cases), exams are based on a specific set of topics and skills. Firstly, find out which exam board will be setting your exam. They provide specifications for each of the exams they set. These are easily accessible from a quick internet search if you haven't been given one by your teacher.

Use this as the basis for what you'll revise in terms of themes and topics. You should also make sure you know what skills will be tested too. For example, will you need to be able to draw graphs? Will you need to extract information from a passage of text? How about arguing a particular viewpoint?

Organise your coursework

When it comes to revising for exams, preparation is key. One of the best ways to get organised is to go through all your coursework notes and pull out those that are relevant to your exam. Not everything that you've studied throughout the year will be directly relevant to your tests, so only select the topics are.

You can then arrange your 'exam' notes in a new folder, so that they're easily accessible should you need to check anything. This condensed version of your coursework can also be useful reading material in the hours leading up to your exam, to familiarise yourself with the content and get you in the right mind-set for the test.

Create a revision timetable

Once you know what you'll be tested on, how can you guarantee that you'll actually put the time and effort in? One of the best ways to revise is to use a revision timetable. Not only do they hold you accountable for studying when you're supposed to, but they can be a great motivator as you mark off each day that you complete.

A revision timetable doesn't need to be elaborate. It can be as simple as a spreadsheet or a written schedule. If you prefer a more technological approach however, why not try a free revision timetable app like Adapt, which calculates the perfect amount of revision for each day. Or, why not try Get Revising's free revision timetable builder?

For those of you who prefer visual learning techniques, using a wall planner as a revision timetable is a great way to

see your entire plan in the one place. If you choose this DIY approach to creating a timetable, then you'll want to:

- Work out how many weeks you have left until each exam.

- Decide how many hours per week you need to study each subject.

- Choose one subject, break up the hours throughout the week and mark on your calendar when you'll study it.

- Try to be as specific as possible with what you'll study. Don't just write the subject name, specify what topics you'll cover and remember to schedule time at the end of each week for practising with specimen papers.

- Do this for each subject and before you know it, you'll have created a personal revision plan to help guide your studying.

Can you explain the content to an eight-year-old?

Make sure you understand all the content. Memorising facts without knowing the context will only get you so far. For application-based questions, you'll need to thoroughly understand the information as well as how it all links together.

If you're not sure whether or not you understand something, try explaining it to an eight-year old (seriously). This might feel like an odd thing to do for GCSE or A Level subjects, but the more you understand something, the simpler you can make it sound when writing it in the exam.

Use a variety of revision techniques

One of the biggest mistakes students make when revising is only using one approach. Sure, you may enjoy reading through textbooks and highlighting notes, but sometimes a more pro-active approach is required to ensure you actually retain the information you're revising. Here are some revision techniques you should use to mix up your approach:

Keyword Recall – Using your exam notes, write out individual keywords and phrases that relate to each topic. You can write them out all on the one page, on flashcards or, better still, on post-it notes. Stick the keywords around the house and every time you see one, try to recall as much information about the topic as you can. It's best to verbalise your thoughts out loud to strengthen your memory.

Student as Teacher – Again, using your exam notes, have a friend or family member choose a topic from your folder. Your role is to act as the teacher, teaching the other person about the subject as if they were the student. This is a good revision technique to improve your confidence as you realise how much you know.

Mind Mapping – Creating mind maps can be a good way of organising key themes or important equations into a visual reminder. Start by writing the subject in the centre of the page and creating stems that connect to each theme or formula. You can then add other relevant information around each theme. This technique works particularly well for visual learners or for creative students that are studying a more logical subject.

Study Groups – Your fellow classmates can be a great source of information, inspiration and support. Joining or organising a study group can provide you with the motivation to revise even when you don't feel like it. In a study group, students can help you with any areas of a subject that you feel stuck with. It also makes revising more fun and you can organise quizzes or competitions to keep things interesting.

Analyse and practice with past papers

One of the best ways to revise is to analyse past papers. Practising exam questions is great, but if you don't know where you have gained or lost marks, then you'll likely make the same mistakes in the next test too.

Take the time to read the mark scheme. Find out which words and phrases the exam board give marks for and which ones lose you marks. Okay, so this can be a bit time consuming, but it's definitely a much more efficient use of your time than just reading through notes, and hoping for the best.

Once you know how points are awarded, it's time to get down to business. Gather all the past exam papers that you can from your exam board's website (useful links at the end of this section) and work your way through them one-by-one.

As your exam approaches, start to tackle full papers in one go, under exam conditions and within the allowed time frame. This will improve your exam technique, get you used to answering questions under pressure and improve your time management skills.

If you've exhausted all the past papers in your subject, you can also try practising with specimen papers that are created by education companies and designed in the same style as those from the exam boards.

Don't overdo it - schedule regular breaks

As the saying goes, 'all work and no play, makes Jack a dull boy'. It's important to take regular breaks when you're revising for exams. It can be tempting to continue revising for long hours when you feel in the mood, but it's actually best to stop at the point that you feel you're 'in the flow'. If you take a break when you're feeling engaged, you'll find it much easier to get back into the swing of things when you go back to it.

One way to make sure you don't overdo it with long periods of study is to use the Pomodoro technique. Essentially, this involves setting a timer for half-hour periods and working without distraction until the buzzer sounds. You can then take a ten or fifteen-minute break until you set the timer again.

Now go forth, conquer that revision and smash those exams!

What do you think? What is the best way to revise?

15 February, 2020

Study motivation

Skipping seminars to stay in bed? Can't seem to stay focused? Here's how to avoid sleepwalking through your studies and get motivated.

By Holly Turner

How can I motivate myself?

Get your work done properly, and you can kick back with a clear conscience. Here's how you get yourself started.

Create the space

Wherever you live, be it halls of residence or shared accommodation, establish a work area. Even if you don't have a desk, restricting a small area just for learning will help create boundaries between work and play.

Ditch the distraction

Consider your working environment and cut out anything that tempts you from the task at hand, such as TV – or even music. If you just can't work in silence, go for tunes without vocals.

Establish a work schedule

Break up the slog into more manageable sessions. So, if you're faced with six hours worth of work, for example, why not split it into three two-hour sessions? You'll feel like you've achieved something faster which is a buzz that'll keep you going.

Create regular breaks and rewards

There's nothing like the prospect of a treat to keep you focused, so be sure to pepper your sessions with them. Five minutes free time every hour, for example, will help to maintain that spark and drive. Use the opportunity to leave your working environment, get some fresh air, or do something rewarding. If you're organised enough you can keep the weekends free too, so you can look forward to a night out on Friday.

Study effectively

There's no point reading a textbook if you know you're not taking it in. Think about how you learn best and try different things.

Why do I procrastinate?

If you're hoping to give yourself a kick up the arse, begin by understanding why you've lost momentum in the first place. Only you can decide what's behind your lack of motivation attitude, but here are some of the main offenders:

♦ Lack of focus – any long-term goals, like graduating, don't register

♦ Lack of interest – your coursework leaves you cold

♦ Lack of drive – you're not good at working under your own steam

Other factors can include stress, depression, the break-up of a relationship, or problems with drink or drugs. The key is to highlight what's holding you back in order to take steps to overcome the situation.

Share the problem

There's no shame in admitting you're having issues focusing. In many ways, it takes courage to admit the only time you get your head down is when it hits the pillow. What's more, people will want to help. Whether it's a good friend, a course tutor or your student welfare officer, they can help you get back on track. But first, of course, you have to want to help yourself.

25 May 2021

How to make a revision timetable

Having a schedule while you revise will allow you to effectively cover all you need to study. Read about how to make a revision timetable.

By Jamie Dobbs

Prioritise topics

Before creating your revision timetable, decide which subjects you're strongest at and which are your weakest. Outlining this before you start revising will give you oversight into what topics you need to spend a bit more time on.

Divide time appropriately

Once you've outlined which topics you'll need to spend more time on, reflect this in your revision timetable. Allocate more time to any subjects you feel less confident about. Do remember to still make time to cover topics that you're feeling confident about. What's important is that you revise each topic but be smart about the time allocated to each.

Chunk subjects

Split each subject you plan to study into separate chunks. This will allow you to separate the subjects that you don't need to spend as much time revising from those you do. You'll also get an overview of how many topics you need to cover and how much time you should be allocating to each.

Colour-code subjects

Representing each subject in your revision timetable with a different colour will provide a better visual overview of your study. At a glance you can easily see what's coming up. You can check that you're spending the right amount of time per subject and pinpoint which topics you need to allocate more time to.

Schedule breaks

Divide your study time up with appropriate breaks. Short breaks every 30 to 35 minutes will allow you to vary what you study throughout the day. You'll be able to approach each topic with a fresh mind and not feel burnt out after a few hours. Stepping away from your study and coming back with a clear head can also help with problem solving.

Fit around your daily life

Your daily life shouldn't be put on hold because you're revising. It's important that you create a revision timetable that considers your usual daily activities. Scheduling these into your timetable will provide balance and give you the chance to take breaks when you need.

Be flexible

Studying a topic for less time than you intended or missing a study session isn't the end of the world. Life happens and a revision timetable should account for that. Leave room in your timetable for flexibility in case you need to move some topics around. You might also find that on some days, you have more energy and motivation than others.

Try going digital

You might prefer crafting a hand drawn revision timetable, and that's OK. But you may find a digital one more convenient. Using the calendar in your phone, your email or any timetable app will mean you always have your revision timetable with you. When you need to be flexible, it's also a lot easier to make changes to a digital version of your timetable than a written one.

Key Facts

- According to Which, sixth forms see your GCSE performance as an indicator of how well you'll do in your A-levels or other, advanced studies, and use a scoring system based on your grades to predict how well you are likely to do. (page 2)

- For some intermediate apprenticeships or traineeships, you don't need to have certain grades at all – instead, you may just need to show that you have the skills through things like work experience and volunteering. (page 2)

- Students are graded on a numerical system from 9 to 1, rather than from A to E, after the system changed from letters to numbers in 2018. (page 3)

- The English Baccalaureate (EBacc) is a measure for schools which shows how many students take a number of set subjects (English, maths, history or geography, the sciences and a language) and their average results. (page 4)

- Alongside GCSEs, you can study for work-related qualifications, also called vocational qualifications or Technical Awards. They can help you develop practical skills in subjects such as construction, computing and childcare. (page 4)

- In the UK, there are 'core' and 'foundation' subjects that all key stage 4 students must take. Maths, English, and science are the core subjects, and IT/computing, physical education, and citizenship are the foundations. (page 5)

- Most students take around 9 GCSEs or equivalent. (page 8)

- Scottish Highers are the Scottish equivalent to A-Levels. (page 12)

- A Levels are academic and general qualifications and Applied General Qualifications are courses that are about a vocational area and more practical. T Levels are technical qualifications, equivalent to 3 A Levels that combine classroom study and work placements and train you to do a job. (page 14)

- Over 300,000 young people chose to do A Levels last year. (page 14)

- Over 200,000 young people chose to study a Level 3 vocational qualification last year. (page 15)

- There are over 160 universities in the UK. (page 24)

- In England, an undergraduate university degree will cost you a maximum of £9,250 per year. (page 29)

- In Wales, you will be charged up to £9,000 for home students and £3,925 for EU and Northern Irish students. Students in Northern Ireland will be charged up to £4,030 for home students and £9,250 for students from elsewhere in the UK. (page 29)

- In Scotland you will not be charged if you are from Scotland, or the EU, although students from England, Wales or Northern Ireland will be expected to pay up to £9,250. (page 29)

- Whilst undertaking an apprenticeship in the UK, you will earn the following; if you are under 19, this will be £3.90 per hour minimum. If you're over 19, this will be the National Minimum Wage. (page 29)

- Apprentices are also entitled to 21 days paid holiday plus bank holidays in the UK. (page 30)

- 92% of apprentices go on to secure employment or go on to further study after completing their training. (page 31)

A-levels

These are qualifications usually taken by students aged 16 to 18 at schools and sixth-form colleges, although they can be taken at any time by school leavers at local colleges or through distance learning. They provide an accepted route to degree courses and university and usually take two years to complete.

Apprenticeship

A form of vocational training which involves learning a trade or skill through working. An apprentice will often shadow an experienced practitioner of a trade, learning the occupation 'on the job'. Some apprenticeships can take many years.

Career College

Career Colleges are schools designed to provide vocational education. This means that students will learn and develop skills necessary to perform particular jobs.

Degree

An honours degree is the most common qualification awarded on graduation from university. It is graded according to classification: first class (a `first`), upper second class (2:1), lower second class (2:2), third class (a `third`) and fail.

Exam Stress

A feeling of nervousness, fear or worry before or during a test.

Further education

Education for 16- to 18-year-olds, for example college or sixth form.

Gap year

A year away from study or full-time employment, usually taken before starting university or after graduating. Gap years can help students to broaden their horizons through travel or volunteering.

Graduate

Someone who has studied for and been awarded a degree.

Halls of residence

Most new students live in accommodation provided by the university, called halls of residence.

Higher education (HE)

Post-18 education, usually provided by a university and leading to the award of a degree or postgraduate qualification. There are currently over two million higher education students in the UK.

IGCSE

Introduced in 1988, International GCSE is an alternative to the traditional GCSEs, offered by Cambridge and Edexcel exam boards.

National Curriculum

The statutory set of guidelines set down by the Government which determine the subject material and attainment targets taught in schools in England and Wales. The National Curriculum applies to pupils up to the age of 16.

Postgraduate

A postgraduate is a student who has completed a degree and gone on to further academic study, such as a PhD or a Masters course.

State school

A school which is funded and run by the Government, at no cost to the pupils. An independent school, on the other hand, is one which is privately run and which pupils pay a fee to attend. These are sometimes known as 'private schools' or 'public schools' (please note, not all private schools are public schools).

Student debt

A higher education student can apply for a student loan from the Government, which they begin paying back monthly after graduation once they are earning a certain salary. They may also incur additional debts such as overdrafts while at university.

Student loan

A sum of money lent to students by the government in order to pay for their tuition and maintenance fees. It is paid back gradually once the graduate is earning over £21,000 per year.

Students' union

Every university has a students' union: an organisation that is run by students, for students. Student unions usually offer a variety of social and sporting opportunities as well as practical services such as help groups and advice centres.

Tuition fees

The amount of money charged by a university or college for the course of study they are providing.

UCAS

UCAS stands for Universities and Colleges Admissions Service. Anyone who wants to study an undergraduate degree in the UK will have to apply through UCAS.

Undergraduate

An undergraduate is a term applied to a student studying towards a first degree but who has not yet graduated.

Vocational

A qualification which is relevant to a particular career and can be expected to provide a route into that career.

Vocational learning

Education that provides practical training for a specific occupation or vocation, for example agriculture, carpentry or beauty therapy. Traditionally this is delivered through 'hands-on' experience rather than academic learning, although there may be a combination of these elements depending on the course.

Activities

Brainstorm

♦ Create a mindmap of all the different options available to you for GCSE/A-Level.

♦ Create a mindmap of careers that you may be interested in doing in the future. Do you need to do a degree or apprenticeship to do that job?

♦ In small groups, brainstorm things to consider when choosing a course at college or university.

Research

♦ Conduct a survey amongst your class mates. How many of them are considering going to university? Are any considering an apprenticeship or an alterative?

♦ In small groups, do some research into different universities in the UK. What are the differences in the types of course each one offers? Write a report on your findings and share with your class.

♦ Do some research into student loans. Who is entitled to a loan? How do you apply for a student loan? How much would you receive? How and when would you pay it back? Write a report and share with the rest of your class.

♦ In pairs, do some research into apprenticeships in the UK. You should consider the types of apprenticeships on offer, the benefits they offer and the pay apprentices might receive. How long might an apprenticeship last? Write a short report on your findings.

♦ Do some research into jobs that you may be interested in doing in the future. Do you need any qualifications for this job? If so, where and how can you obtain them? Write your findings down and share with your class.

♦ Create a questionnaire to find out what your peers are interested in studying for their GCSEs or A-Levels. Which are the most popular subjects? Present your findings in a graph.

Design

♦ Imagine you work for a university and have been asked to design a poster to advertise its facilities. It should inform students what it has to offer and encourage them to apply for a place there. Tell them why your university is the one to go for.

♦ Produce a leaflet about student loans. It should provide as much information as possible, including how to apply for a loan.

♦ In pairs, design a leaflet which would help students to budget. Your leaflet should give practical advice on how students can manage their money.

♦ Choose an article from this topic and design an illustration highlighting its key points.

♦ Design a revision planner – what things can you include to help your revision?

♦ Design a poster to help students when making decisions about choosing a subject to study.

♦ Design a infographic for one of the articles in this book.

♦ Design a leaflet for students struggling with exam stress. Be sure to include tips that can help them be successful in their exams.

Oral

♦ In pairs, one of you should play the role of a student who wants to go to university and the other one should try to persuade them that an apprenticeship would be better. Then reverse roles.

♦ In pairs, go through this book and discuss the cartoons you come across. Think about what the artist was trying to portray with each illustration.

♦ Interview some friends and people you know who are older than you. Find out how many of them went to university. How many of them went straight out to work? Ask them the reasons they made the choices they made. Write some notes on your findings and feedback to the rest of the class.

♦ As a class, discuss the differences between going to university or doing an apprenticeship.

Reading/Writing

♦ Write a one-paragraph definition of the word 'apprenticeship' and then compare it with a classmate's.

♦ Imagine you are an Agony Aunt/Uncle and have received a letter from a teen saying their parents are pressurising them to go to university. They do not want to go but feel if they do not they will let them down. Write a suitable reply.

♦ Create a revision timetable.

♦ Write a plan for your personal statement, then do a first draft and get a friend or relative to read it through and suggest changes or improvements. Remember to use the tips in the article 'How to write a personal statement for university' on page 26.

Acknowledgements

The publisher is grateful for permission to reproduce the material in this book. While every care has been taken to trace and acknowledge copyright, the publisher tenders its apology for any accidental infringement or where copyright has proved untraceable. The publisher would be pleased to come to a suitable arrangement in any such case with the rightful owner.

The material reproduced in **issues** books is provided as an educational resource only. The views, opinions and information contained within reprinted material in **issues** books do not necessarily represent those of Independence Educational Publishers and its employees.

Images
Cover image courtesy of iStock. All other images courtesy Freepik, Pixabay & Unsplash.

Illustrations
Simon Kneebone: pages 26, 36 & 38. Angelo Madrid: pages 7, 8 & 19.

Additional acknowledgements
With thanks to the Independence team: Shelley Baldry, Jackie Staines and Tracy Biram

Danielle Lobban

Cambridge, January 2022